# 11 OAK STREET

Graham Cook

# 11 OAK STREET

Graham Cook

ISBN: 978-19041810-0-2

'11 Oak Street' is published by **WRITERSWORLD**, and is produced entirely in the UK. It is available to order from most bookshops in the United Kingdom, and is also globally available via UK-based Internet book retailers.

Fifth Edition

Copy edited by Sue Croft

Cover design by Jag Lall and Charles Leveroni

www.writersworld.co.uk
WRITERSWORLD
2 Bear Close Flats
Bear Close
Woodstock
Oxfordshire
OX20 1JX
England

☎ 01993 812500
☎ 0044 1993 812500

The text pages of this book are produced via an independent certification process that ensures the trees from which the paper is produced come from well-managed sources that exclude the risk of using illegally logged timber while leaving options to use post-consumer recycled paper as well.

# DEDICATION

This book is dedicated to a plethora of people who helped me through all the setbacks that came my way, and to the backbone of my late father, Geoffrey Gordon Cook, DSM, who gave me the moral compass that taught me what was right and what was wrong throughout my life, both in business and private matters.

The thrust of this book is a common problem that permeates our society: the misuse of children by vindictive parents, and the needless consequences of such actions. It is also about corrupt and malevolent lawyers and, sadly, the sometimes cruel hand of fate.

I also dedicate this book to all those who have their backs against the wall; to all those who struggle against overpowering injustice; and to all those wonderful people on the side of the angels who throw them a lifeline.

Last, but not least, I would like to dedicate this book to my late friend and lawyer, Robert Carrow, Esq., one of the most intelligent and well-educated persons I have come across and by far the best lawyer I will ever meet.

1. GROWING UP

2. MY FIRST MARRIAGE

3. MY BUSINESS EMPIRE

4. MY SECOND MARRIAGE

5. MY LAST UK BUSINESS DEAL

6. MARRIAGE SHOCK

7. THE DUPLICITY OF MY LAWYER,
   URIE WALSH

8. URIE WALSH AND THE SECOND MARRIAGE
   SETTLEMENT AGREEMENT

9. URIE WALSH HAD HIS OWN AGENDA

10. THE ABDUCTION,

11. AFTER THE ABDUCTION

12. MY POSITION WAS SIMPLY HOPELESS

13. THE WARDSHIP PROCEEDINGS IN ENGLAND

14. WHO NEEDS ENEMIES WITH A BROTHER LIKE MINE?

15. IN MARIN COUNTY JAIL

16. OUT OF JAIL

17. THE LAW IN SMALL COUNTIES LIKE NAPA

18. IN LIMBO

19. BARBARA'S MODUS OPERANDI

20. KATIE

21. ANN AND LOUISE

22. THE LEGAL MALPRACTICE LAWSUIT

23.   AN IDYLLIC INTERLUDE

24.   WINSTON'S

25.   ANOTHER KAFKAESQUE NIGHTMARE

26.   *THE NAPA SENTINEL*

27.   BOGUS PROSECUTION

28.   THE WINSTON'S TRIAL

29.   VEXATIOUS LITIGANT PROCEEDINGS

30.   KEEPING A ROOF OVER MY HEAD

31.   THINGS YOU NEVER FORGET

32.   TIME TO CALL IT A DAY IN CALIFORNIA

33.   OFF TO SPAIN

34.   EPILOGUE

      APPENDIX 1:
      THE MUTUAL RESTRAINING ORDER UNDER WHICH I
      WAS PROSECUTED IN THE TESS FRANCIS TRIAL

      APPENDIX 2:
      THE COURT TRANSCRIPT OF THE HEARING WHERE I
      WAS DECLARED A VEXATIOUS LITIGANT

      APPENDIX 3:
      LETTER FROM MY LAWYER TO THE COURT
      FOLLOWING THE VEXATIOUS LITIGANT JUDGMENT

      APPENDIX 4:
      MY LETTERS TO THE PRESIDING JUDGE ASKING TO
      BE REMOVED FROM THE VEXATIOUS LITIGANT LIST
      IN CALIFORNIA

# GROWING UP

I have thought long and hard about whether my childhood is relevant to the underlying subject of this book and have determined that it is indeed very relevant. I recently heard a radio interview with one of Britain's top female athletes who said that what spurred her on in the 2012 Olympics was her family in the stadium cheering her on. Unfortunately I just never had that type of family.

I was born in Gosport, Hampshire, England, on 24 September 1949, and grew up in Oxford, living in a council house. I was one of six children and came from what would be termed today a dysfunctional family. First there was my eldest brother. Then there was David. I came next, followed by Robert. Alison, the only sister, died of cancer at the age of thirty. The sixth child was Andrew, who is just like my dear Dad.

My life, as it turned out, was predicated on an appalling lie. Or as a therapist would say to me years later, "My, Mr Cook, your whole life has been built on sand."

I did not particularly enjoy the academic side of school as I found timetables and routine irksome, although I did well—in fact so well that I passed the 11-plus exam to go to the local grammar school, which could of course have led to university. But as I found out much later, my mother lied to me about this and told my school that she didn't think I was suitable for a grammar school education.

We never had any money and my whole childhood was permeated with the sounds of my mother and father arguing about money—which could have been mitigated had my parents not been covering up the massive lie that predated my birth.

In our home was this person, my 'eldest' brother, who made my entire childhood miserable. He would not have anything to do with me in the home and would walk straight past without a word if we met in the street. He went to Oxford Grammar School and was required to leave. He then turned up at my school, where I was happy with my group of friends, and for the whole time he did not speak to me. His attitude towards me pervaded even my early working life. For example, when as a youth I went out drinking in the city of Oxford, he would walk right past without speaking to me. In fact he would stop and talk to people who stood next to me, but it was as if I never existed.

After leaving school, my brother chose a unique career path in that he became a major amphetamine dealer. Inevitably, in time he was caught by the police. During this period I was working hard completing my apprenticeship, and these are some of the headlines that appeared in the local newspaper, the *Oxford Mail*, in regards to him:

**YOUTHS FINED FOR SMASHING SAILING BOAT; ROSE-HILL YOUTH LOSES APPEAL; BAIL MAN GAVE HIMSELF UP; OXFORD MAN ON DRUG CHARGE; DRUGS ARE FOUND AFTER CAR CRASH, COURT TOLD; FEAR FOR GIRL WITNESSES IN DRUGS HEARING; OXFORD MEN ON DRUGS CHARGES; DRUG CHARGE YOUTHS HELD.**

I have quoted only the articles that appeared in the *Oxford Mail* as they were the ones that affected my daily life in my formative years. Having our name in the paper was a stigma that all the family had to bear. My brother was the talk of the town and many assumed I must be tarred with the same brush.

The marriage between my mother and father was simply awful. My father could do no right, and neither could I, and the person who I believed was my eldest brother could do no wrong. I spent my childhood, in fact all my life, being put down by my mother, and to this day I suffer from the emotional abuse she heaped on me. I did not understand why she treated me as she did until I was in my fifties.

My biggest problem today, on account of my mother's attitude towards me, is that it has caused permanent damage to my emotional makeup, quite apart from creating a dysfunctional and divided family. Because of the deep dark numbness that is always at my core, I always feel that, no matter how successful I am, there is bound to be a negative floating around in the background. This stems from a lifetime of my mother's emotional battering and the unhealthy relationship with my eldest brother. In consequence I am gripped by the belief that disaster lurks round every corner.

Nonetheless, this upbringing, however dismal, provided three fundamental and positive influences on my outlook on life, both then and to this day. The first was on account of being so poor and having to wear second-hand and ill-fitting clothes at school, where some of the kids would call me 'Raggy Dan'. This did two things for my character. It helped to create in me compassion and sympathy for people less fortunate than me, and it taught me that the only way to get above the poverty line was to work. From the earliest opportunity I did two paper rounds a day, and in the rest of my spare time earned money grass-cutting and doing whatever other jobs I could get in the neighbourhood. This enabled me to buy nicer clothes (I have always liked to look good) and pay for school trips.

The second influence was my father. He was a very handsome man and both very kind and incredibly honest. He was also an extremely courageous and highly decorated war hero. I grew up looking with pride at his beautiful Royal Marines uniform in his bedroom closet. I am sure that my frequent references to my father's experiences in the Royal Marines were a factor much later in life when my son was sufficiently motivated to join the United States Marine Corps. I have tried in every way to emulate my father's stance and his principles and to be a moral and compassionate being in my turn.

He was my role model in my formative years, and one day he taught me a lesson I've never forgotten. When I was about fourteen he discovered that I had at home a stolen tyre pump I had taken from a bicycle chained alongside others at the open-air swimming pool that my brothers and I used almost daily in the summer months. This was because I wanted to be able to cycle there and back as it was about five miles away from home. He marched me all the way to the swimming pool and made me apologise personally to the person in charge (I didn't know whose bike I stole it from), and for the rest of the summer as a punishment I had always to stay within immediate sight of the pool attendant. With my father, wrong was never right.

The third influence on my life was a film I first saw when I was eleven years old. The film was *High Noon* starring Gary Cooper. As said in an article in *The Telegraph* in August 2003, it is the film most requested by presidents of the United States of America, according to the official White House projectionist. Bill Clinton watched this picture of a marshal deserted by friends and facing outlaws in an against-the-odds showdown a record thirty times; Dwight Eisenhower loved the film and asked for three screenings; and George W Bush saw it at least once. The theme is simple: you have to stand up and be counted even when you put yourself at risk; if you start to run from a problem you will always be running; and there are times in life when you have to make a stand and fight without sacrificing your principles or your morals. I believe this film is without doubt the greatest film ever made and, to this day, if I need to find some backbone, I will watch it so as to build up my fortitude.

I left school at fifteen to do a four-year apprenticeship, and achieved my City & Guilds qualifications as a Heating & Ventilation Engineer, a job I loved. I had always enjoyed working with my hands and resolving practical difficulties, and I liked to think I was carrying out work to a high standard. My job also brought me a dawning awareness of a world I had not known. We did a lot of work in wealthy people's homes, and a desire grew in me to live like that too. However, I figured that the way to make money was to work for it, which definitely did not include, like that elder brother of mine, criminal activity. I eventually went into business for myself and it appeared I had the golden touch, as everything I did brought success after success.

# MY FIRST MARRIAGE

## Chapter 2

At the age of nineteen I came home in the early hours of the morning in the middle of winter to find not only had my parents locked me out, but my personal possessions were scattered all over the front lawn: I had been dating a woman they disapproved of. After sleeping in my car for the first night, I rented a seedy, freezing bedsit at the top of an old Victorian house. One day, while I was working on the heating system in her flat, I met the woman who would become my first wife, Jane. She was a secretary, four years older than me. In due course we got married and rented a small flat. My mother refused to come to the wedding, saying I should not be marrying at second hand (Jane had been married before). After a year or two we moved to the exclusive community of Rock, near Wadebridge in Cornwall.

Ann and Louise are our twin daughters. I was present at their birth. They were born premature and very tiny, and when they left hospital after many weeks, for the first six months or so I would literally sit up all night watching them.

We were happy except for one thing: Jane's obsessive and baseless jealousy. When we were first married, if I so much as talked to my sister-in-law, she would create rows. When we moved to the first home we bought, if I spoke to the wife of our next-door neighbour she would create rows. When we moved to Rock in Cornwall, if I spoke to the neighbour on the left or the neighbour and her daughter across the road or the neighbour to the right across the road, she would create rows. If I waved to my lawyer's secretary as our cars passed, she would create rows. But however alarmingly she carried on I never rowed back—it was impossible anyway to get so much as a word in—consequently, I would escape to the silence of my van.

It was the same when we moved to Bristol. If I spoke to my neighbour's daughters—more rows, and even though I had neither the time nor the inclination to have an affair with anyone, even so I was accused of having an affair with my happily married secretary, who was twenty years older than me. Life became impossible and we divorced. Of course, if you know about psychological projection, you will be able to guess who in fact was having the affair.

From the start, when we separated in 1978, Jane used Ann and Louise as a weapon of vengeance. They lived just seven miles away and on occasion she would rent expensive cars to keep on her drive just to try and make me jealous. I had to get a court order to force her to take my child-support payments and had to go to court each time I wanted to take Ann and Louise on vacation outside the United Kingdom (which the court would always permit). Unsatisfactory as it was, I had access every other weekend and I could cope with the situation because I was now wealthy and if necessary I could afford to pay lawyers.

A situation came about where I heard rumours that Jane's soon-to-be third husband was going around telling people he was marrying into money. Now you may or may not think this right, but as he would be stepfather to my daughters I decided to run a background check on him using the services of a well-known ex-Scotland Yard policeman, now a private detective. I met with him in a public house in Shirehampton near Bristol, and when I saw the file on this man it made shocking reading. Unfortunately, because of the way the information was obtained, I could not use it in any proceedings for a change of custody from their mother to me. I also discovered that he was not seeing his children by his first marriage or paying his child support, and his first wife was living in miserable circumstances doing the best she could to raise their children on her own.

When Jane married him she made life as difficult as possible for me. When I went to pick up my daughters at weekends I would have to sit and wait in my car until the exact time designated by my court order. Those children dared not show any affection towards me until they were out of their mother's sight. Against her own lawyer's advice, Ann and Louise were forced to call the stepfather 'Daddy'.

It was obviously Jane's intention to do her utmost to try and alienate Anne and Louise from me: my punishment for leaving her.

# MY BUSINESS EMPIRE

## Chapter 3

When Jane and I moved to Rock, despite having virtually no capital, I started my own business, aged twenty-three, installing heating systems. My new career, however, nearly came to an immediate and final end when I was due to start installing the heating in the boarding house of a battleaxe of a landlady called Mrs Mole. I always made a promise to my clients that I would start the day we had agreed on and finish the day I said I would: this was my business mantra. On the day I was due to start Mrs Mole's work I had a phone call from the local representative of Shell Oil, who wanted to inspect a past heating system I had done. The inspection was to be on the same day I was due to start installing at Mrs Mole's, so I turned up at her house full of fear and trepidation, knowing I had to tell her I would have to leave a few hours after starting.

Talk about 'more haste less speed'! In my anxiety to get the job done I accidently tripped over her phone cable and smashed the glass in one of her interior doors. I cleared up this mess then departed in haste in my car to meet with the Shell representative. Alas, my car skidded and the front end went over the nearby cliff that ran alongside the road. As it was balancing precariously over the steep drop, I managed to scramble into the back of the car, but my dog Sally kept jumping from the back to the front and then back again, which shook both the car and me. Fortunately, two passers-by came to the rescue and, having got me and the dog out, we all sat on the boot lid until the tow truck came and hauled the car back to safety.

I turned up to my meeting with the Shell representative, though late, passed my inspection and thereafter got lots of work installing oil-fired heating systems for Shell Oil clients. Mrs Mole was happy too.

It is often asked how entrepreneurs make their money. The answer is simple: they see a situation and then go about exploiting it, which is exactly what I did. The worldwide oil crisis struck and, all of a sudden, work involving oil-fired heating just dried up. One day a double glazing salesman came to my home, and as he sat on my couch trying to sell me a double glazing system to save energy, he mentioned to me in passing that everyone was getting into the cavity wall insulation market, i.e. filling the gaps between the outer and inner walls of people's houses to make their homes more fuel efficient.

Being young and impetuous but seeing the opportunity here, I sold everything I could, including my car, and went on a cavity wall insulation course, buying a van and all the requisite equipment. At weekends, along with Jane, I went throughout our extended locality putting leaflets and brochures through people's letter boxes with a free-reply business card. At nights I put on my suit and went out as a salesman selling the insulation, then during the day I exchanged the suit for overalls and installed the insulation I had sold!

The business grew and I began to take on installation staff and build up a sales force. I soon converted my initial business, Graham Cook (Heating Services Ltd), to this one, which I called Cosyworld, and built into it the same quality and work ethic that was second to none. The business continued to expand hugely—and then came my big break; I won a huge government contract to insulate the walls and roofs of dozens upon dozens of government buildings and military camps throughout the south of England. This turned into a contract to insulate tens upon tens of thousands of houses owned by the military throughout the same area.

There was, however, a problem getting this particular contract in that a letter came the last working day before Christmas requiring a good bank reference to clinch the deal. This bank reference, moreover, had to be in the first working day after the Christmas break. What did I do? I persuaded my bank manager to open up his branch that Christmas Day and begged and pleaded for that bank reference. As I was leaving his office, reference in hand, I always remember what he said to me: "Graham, if you die, I am coming to your funeral to make sure they screw down the coffin lid!" I turned up with the bank reference and got the contract.

I had now become a major employer, employing hundreds of insulators and running a huge commission-only sales force with depots all over the area and a fleet of vehicles. Things progressed so well that we became one of the largest insulation contractors in the UK, doing work for all sorts of major clients, large house builders and hospitals, all the time increasing our logistical reach and range of insulation products right up to insulating very large heated oil-storage tanks.

As to the original government contract, years into it my secretary received a phone call one day from the Chief Quantity Surveyor of this particular government department telling her, "I want to see Graham Cook in my office at ten o'clock today." I did not know what to make of this message, and with a fair degree of anxiety went off to meet with this person who was absolutely critical to the success of my business. As I entered his office he put his hand out to shake mine and said, "Mr Cook, I am retiring today and I wanted to tell you personally that the contract you have with us is the best-run contract I have ever administered. I just wanted to say thank you".

One of the reasons for the success of my various companies was that I always employed people for senior management positions who were more than competent, and I retained their management services by the considerate way I treated them and the exceptional perks they received. I made a point of always doing the first of a three-interview process myself, as well as the last—this was because I wanted to make sure that the staff who were doing the second interview did not recruit people below the level of competence of my senior managers simply so they would not be a threat to their own career. As to the third interview, I would invite all of the persons involved in the interview process, including the spouse of the interviewee if appropriate, to attend. The purpose of this was so we could make sure every iota of the management role was understood. Then to get things off to a good start for successful candidates, we invited them to take their spouses to dine at the restaurant of their choice and we would pick up the tab. I never once lost a single member of staff to another company. There was never any backbiting, and I can truthfully write that I ran very happy, progressive companies. In fact we were years ahead of our time as regards working conditions and dealing with our employees.

Having a successful business career enabled me to generate all sorts of ways to benefit those less fortunate than me over and above ensuring that all my staff had excellent salaries, security of employment and the best possible working equipment and vehicles. For the staff I set up a system whereby any of them could obtain a loan from the company and, although I owned the company, I would never know they had borrowed money. I was also able to disperse the company's wealth amongst not just the staff but also outsiders, which gave me a lot of personal satisfaction. We raised money throughout the year from voluntary contributions from the staff/employees, which I agreed to double. The money was collected to deliver Christmas food parcels via rented vans to those persons throughout the West Country who we found out had slipped through the welfare net. Every year it was the same argument from my fellow directors as to why we *rented* vans when we had so many of our own. My answer was always the same: if we used our vans, painted all over with our livery, we would look as if we were doing this to boost our company's reputation.

One of the other things I was able to do, having total control over my company, was to indulge my socialist leanings along with my capitalist principles. In a landmark decision involving this, my first major company, I decided we should employ staff in proportion to the ethnic mix of the United Kingdom and I threw down the gauntlet to all and sundry that this would become part of our hiring policy. When announcing this at one of our depots one Friday, I came up against a brick wall, with the entire outside staff wanting to stay white and male (remember this was years ago and the discrimination laws that exist now were yet to come). Faced with this head-on opposition I asked my secretary, who was present, if she had her handbag with her, and when she produced it told her to go round and collect the company vehicle keys as we would start hiring again on the Monday. My strategy had the desired effect and my policy was of course an ongoing success.

Considering that I had made a substantial fortune over the years, in this and my previous business, what I was most proud of was that I had done it all ethically: from day one I gave my employees six weeks' paid leave plus statutory holidays; paid more in salaries than the industry norms; never hired 'n' fired as was common in this industry; and made sure all my employees had the very best safety equipment, tools, vehicles etc. I had excellent relationships with my employees and staff, who were simply not intimidated by me, as the following story indicates.

One day I arrived at my Bristol offices and saw one of my vehicles with the boot open and all the equipment showing, which made it very easy for a passer-by to steal something. So as to prove a point, I put some of the equipment on the car park floor and after I had entered our offices told the respective employee to go and take a look at his vehicle—not telling him what I had done. When he came back into the offices he was not best pleased.

When I left my office later, as I was walking across the car park I noticed the boot lid of my Jaguar was up and the spare wheel, boot carpet, golf bag etc. were on the car park floor. As I reached the car I could see a note left in the boot, from the selfsame employee, pointing out that by leaving my boot unlocked I was in violation of our company property policy. Of course, he was right! And not only was he right, more importantly it showed he was not afraid to have a joke at my expense.

After I had sold my first company and remunerated the twins' mother handsomely with the money I had left, I bought the home pictured on the next page, along with twenty-six acres of unspoilt views, a six-car garage, stables for four horses and a six-acre cider apple orchard. I had the house furnished from top to bottom by the very best interior designer as well as having it decorated inside and out to the highest possible specification. I also added a swimming pool. As well as this I had the best housekeeper you could wish for, who would come in three days a week to keep my home spotless.

# MY SECOND MARRIAGE

## Chapter 4

I had money, a holiday coming up, and a dear friend and business colleague, George Allen, living in the suburbs of Richmond, Virginia, in the United States. So off I went, in November 1980, thirty-one years old, with my handmade suits, shirts, shoes, Rolex watch and English accent—all the requisite accoutrements for precipitating what occurred at the end of my spur-of-the-moment first visit to the United States. George Allen would be out of town for a few days and as I had not met his wife I did not want to stay at his home while he was away. I checked into the Hyatt Regency Hotel, which was like paradise on earth for a single man: there was a nurses' conference running and the hotel was full.

When George came back I stayed at his home for a few days. He then had to travel again on business so I decided to drive down to Fort Lauderdale, Florida, where George would join me later. When I reached Fort Lauderdale I came across yet another paradise: it was Secretaries' Week, so again I was not short of companionship. George and I met up and spent a few days together, after which it was time for him to move on and for me to finish off my travel plans. I took a flight to Palm Springs, California, and checked into the Sheraton Plaza.

It was here that I met Barbara, seven days younger than me. I was lying by the pool at my hotel and what I did not realise in my naivety was that there were women who would check into a cheaper hotel or motel, but sit by the pool of an expensive hotel looking for men with a Rolex and all the other distinguishing features of wealth. I fitted the bill exactly. We got talking. Then one evening, on Thanksgiving, Barbara came up to me in the hotel restaurant as I was having dinner and asked if she could buy me a drink. Two other women did the same, but Barbara was the one I had previously met and been attracted to, and so the story begins.

People have asked what I saw in Barbara; what made me fall in love with the only woman I have ever really been in love with. An impossible question with an impossible answer, I guess. Apart from being extremely attractive and our having a terrific sex life, she had a great personality too—sparkling, witty, vivacious, attentive . . . The catch in all this was that the woman I thought I had married was not in fact the woman I actually married.

When we met she was working as a part-time secretary at a fire station in Tiburon in California. A relationship developed, each of us commuting between her home in Sausalito, California and my home in Bristol. Those were the days of cheap standby flights so I could easily fly from Heathrow to San Francisco, departing on a Friday and returning the following Tuesday, with Barbara reciprocating, although generally her stays with me in England were longer.

She became my second wife. I sold my house as it was too close to the countryside for Barbara's liking, and bought instead, still in Bristol, a luxury four-bed ground floor apartment, 17 Seawalls, in one of the most exclusive apartment complexes outside of London.

When we decided to marry there was a problem to be resolved, namely, what would we do about Tripp, her three-year-old son by her first marriage, of whom she had custody. We needed the consent of his father, Fred Parr-Cox (known as Buzz). I was aware that by marrying Barbara I would also be taking on the responsibility of helping to raise him—a slightly daunting prospect as, although he was very young, he was totally out of control. Barbara as a mother was out of her depth and had no way, nor even any inclination, to control him. What I heard and witnessed instilled in me a profound determination, when Barbara and I later separated, to remain involved in raising our own son and to maintain an ongoing relationship with him.

The first thing that astounded me was Tripp's aversion to having his hair washed and he would go for weeks without having it shampooed. Then there was the television situation. Our bedroom was below the living room, and each morning Barbara would get up, go upstairs, turn on the television and allow Tripp to sit watching it. This was not a problem except that every time he wanted the channel changed there would be a pounding on the floor and Barbara would get out of bed and go upstairs to change the channel for him! Unbelievably, she would do this over and over again.

The first time Barbara, Tripp and I travelled to Napa, California, to meet with Barbara's mother, we went to a family restaurant, and because he did not get the meal he wanted Tripp literally swiped everything off the restaurant table and created such a tantrum we had to leave. Then on his first visit to England we went to London and I was astounded when I turned round to see Tripp kicking my father (who had recently had a heart attack). The reason for this was my father would not buy him an ice cream. As to Tripp's diet, it consisted solely of peanut butter and jam sandwiches.

It was arranged that Barbara would meet with Buzz at the Café Trieste in Sausalito to discuss Tripp's going to live in England. The result was he gave his consent. When she told me of his agreement she also told me that he had tears in his eyes, because England was a country that for reasons never explained, he despised. To be sure that he really was at ease with the arrangement I phoned Buzz and suggested I meet with him the next day. What occurred intrigued me: he looked in his golf diary, hunting diary and sailing diary and said, "Graham, I am too busy. You can take the kid." In return for his consent I gave him my word that if I ever severed my business connections in the UK I would reciprocate the arrangement and relocate with his son back to San Francisco. Little did I know his true motivation when he so easily consented to his son going to live in England.

Just after Barbara and I were married and still living in California, I paid for my mother and father and Ann and Louise to visit us, and we all stayed at Barbara's home in Sausalito. One night I had to go into San Francisco to have dinner with a business colleague from my company in England. A trip to California had been his prize for his sales performance. Barbara had declined to come with me and when I was gone she asked my mother, a Roman Catholic, if she could tell her something in the strictest confidence, to which my mother agreed. She confided in her that she was pregnant and had arranged an appointment for the next day at a clinic to have a termination. She swore my mother to secrecy. Naturally, no mother, let alone a Catholic, would keep a secret like that from a son, so when I returned home in the early hours of the morning my mother was waiting up for me and told me all. The next day I waited for Barbara to set off to the clinic and followed her in another car. To this day I can remember sitting at the bottom of the clinic bed begging her not to go through with it. Finally she agreed, and while in England Graham Jnr was born on 22 March 1982. Alas, Barbara never forgave me for stopping her from going ahead with the abortion and in fact when he was about four years old she told one of my brothers, "I will never forgive your brother for getting me pregnant."

This story not only displays a lack of intelligence on Barbara's part as regards reading my mother's character, but also may explain why I became so desperate to maintain close contact with my son.

# MY LAST UK BUSINESS DEAL

## Chapter 5

When I resigned from the job I had running Cosyworld, which I had sold to a subsidiary of Pilkington's Plc, I had no intention of remaining in the insulation industry or re-entering it. However, my successor, whom I had advised against appointing, began to systematically change everything I had built up. There were changes to the salary structures, holiday entitlements, bonus schemes, working vehicle specifications—you name it, he changed it. The consequence was that my former employees were leaving in droves or coming to my home pleading for my help. There was nothing I could do—apart from going back into business again. This I decided to do. However, I had a problem: my employment service agreement contained within the original acquisition deal stated I could not run, manage or control an insulation company for two years unless the company had traded for at least five years. With my lawyers I overcame this problem by buying a company, for £799, that was about to go into liquidation. This company was merely a shell, with no assets or employees, but it had been trading for over five years. So upon acquisition we changed the company's name to Energycare Limited, restructured the share capital and appointed a new board of directors.

I received a letter from Pilkington's Plc, threatening me with legal action if I did not desist. My lawyers responded to this with a simple letter enclosing a copy of Energycare Limited's original Certificate of Incorporation, showing it had been originally registered far beyond the five year period. That was the last we heard from Pilkington's.

My next problem was that I needed an insulation system to market and install for my new company. Fortuitously, one had recently come on the market, developed by a subsidiary of Shell Chemicals Plc known as Thermocomfort Limited. Their system consisted of polystyrene pellets injected into the wall cavities of a building and at the time of injection sprayed with an adhesive so it set in the cavity in slab form. The only difficulty was that I had first been approached by Thermocomfort Limited while I was working as a managing director at Pilkington's. Thermocomfort and I then had to take a gamble—they would need to offer their system to the Pilkington subsidiary, Fibreglass Limited, so we could not be accused of any legal or business impropriety. Fortunately for us, Pilkington's were developing their own rival system and Thermocomfort Limited were literally shown the door. I was in the clear to do a deal.

As Thermocomfort Limited wanted the use of my services, contacts and reservoir of available skilled insulation technicians, I was able to negotiate the deal of the century: Energycare would get the exclusive rights to the Thermocomfort product for the entire south-west of England, plus free enquiries from their national advertising, and no other Thermocomfort contractor could enter our area to do any work. This agreement would be in perpetuity as long as I remained a director of Energycare Limited.

Based, therefore, on the watertight contract I had with Thermocomfort Limited, I opened warehouses throughout the south-west, hired staff and insulation technicians and bought a number of specialist trucks from Thermocomfort to use in the installation of their products.

One of the reasons our sales figures were so good, apart from Energycare Limited having a great reputation, was being able to use the contacts I had made when running my previous company. A lot could also be put down to some of the sales aids we came up with, which were both unique and effective. Here are a couple of examples.

One day I was out playing golf. One of the other golfers was a wholesaler for very expensive, hand-stitched ladies' handbags. As there was a recession and he was going through a very tough time financially, I asked him what he wanted for his stock of handbags. I bought the lot and had them shipped to my Bristol warehouse. I said nothing to my staff in Bristol as to why the warehouse was full of women's handbags and suffered weeks of derision from the staff there before we had the Bristol commission-only sales meeting. At the meeting I produced one of each of the six styles of handbag that my PA had assured me would suit ladies from as young as seventeen to very old ladies. The plan was that each salesperson would carry a stock of the range of handbags and when they entered the prospective client's home would drop them on the living room floor. The salesperson would then tell the wife that if an order was placed at the time, they would leave behind the handbag of her choice. The downside was that in no time we were flooded with orders and ran out of handbags!

I had another idea: the problem with selling insulation products is that there is no pleasing visual end result, and they are not sexy. One day I was in the doctor's surgery and picked up a women's magazine that had a pattern in it for making large beanbags. I had a friend whose girlfriend was starting out making handmade shirts, so what we did was to contract her to make beanbags. They were produced from the very best quality calico, with a double-stitched lining, the Energycare logo tastefully printed on it throughout, and filled with our warm, soft polystyrene beads. The plan was that the commission-only salesperson would drop one of these on the potential client's living room floor with the same sales pitch as the handbags—if they placed the order there and then, they would have the beanbag. This sales aid not only proved the product warm and comfy but also, because they were made to such a high standard, they reflected the service a client of Energycare would receive. There was an added benefit too in that they provided permanent advertising of the Energycare name that reached to clients' friends and neighbours and thus more orders. These beanbags became so successful people would order and pay for them as gifts to family and friends.

All was going well until after a while Thermocomfort Limited figured out they were on the wrong end of the contract. Our sales were meant to be 8% of UK sales and we were making 25%. Also they had signed contracts with other insulation contractors but had not told them they could not do any work in the counties defined in the Energycare contract. Furthermore, the percentage of the free enquiries we were getting from their national advertising that related to our logistical area was costing Thermocomfort more than we were paying them in royalties. Of course, the usual way to resolve these types of problems was to enter into equal, frank and free negotiations, but unfortunately this subsidiary of Shell Chemicals did not operate in this manner. It was run by three pit-bull business types who wanted to tear our contract up and start all over again. I could not do that as my entire Energycare business plan was based on the original Thermocomfort contract.

The last time we met I refused to take their bullying and threats any longer, especially in my own office, and I had them ejected. From then on it was a war of wills. Apart from trying to get out of the Energycare contract, they had other agendas: they wanted use of the company name for access to a huge and highly successful computer software system that we had spent a lot of time in developing and paid a fortune for. We used it to plan and schedule all the orders we were getting, and for paying the commissions to our commission-only sales force. When I would not play their version of doing business, their solution was to cut off the business enquiries in our logistical area and then our supply of raw materials. We now had a war of attrition on our hands and Energycare was being driven into the ground financially.

As if this was not enough, I started to get phone calls out of the blue from people I did not know who were chairpersons of or related to the construction industry in the south-west of England. All of this told me the same basic message: they had been contacted by Thermocomfort's senior management and warned off in case they had any thoughts of a buy-out for Energycare Limited, i.e. Thermocomfort did not want any entity with financial clout and therefore access to lawyers. However, they made one phone call too many. They contacted the SGB Group Plc which had a subsidiary, Peter Cox Limited, who were Thermocomfort contractors, and the next thing I knew, the two most powerful executives of Peter Cox Limited were in my office offering me very substantial unsecured bailout funds which I accepted, until they could acquire Energycare Limited in full, and subsequently did.

I sold Energycare Limited on 9 July 1982, to the SGB Group Plc. At the time the SGB Group was the world's largest scaffolding contractor and I elected to take the money in shares rather than cash as the previous year SGB had won the contract to build all the scaffolding for the Pope's visit to the United Kingdom and the Republic of Ireland: consequently their profits had received a huge boost. Unfortunately, no sooner had the shares been allocated to me than they plummeted in value to half of what they were previously worth. These shares and their subsequent declining value would have a major effect on my circumstances later.

To the pit bulls at Thermocomfort who were used to getting their own way, the acquisition of Energycare by the SGB Group was akin to a declaration of war. They had now been outmanoeuvred twice—once in the agreement I signed with them to market and install their products, and the second time in my selling out to the SGB Group—and they were not about to take this lying down. A business-to-business feud developed between Shell Chemicals Limited and the SGB Group. I was neither directly nor indirectly involved, and although I had done nothing wrong, what happened next would ultimately cost me my marriage to Barbara.

The problem I had was, while I was in the clear legally in regards to the acquisition of Energycare Limited by the SGB Group, there was the clause in the Thermocomfort contract where it became null and void if I ceased to be a director. I could not resign as MD of Energycare Limited because if the contract with Thermocomfort was terminated by them, I would have left myself wide open to be sued by the SGB Group. So resigning was not an option. Now we had a bigger problem. We had a main board director of the SGB Group who insisted he would take charge of negotiations between SGB and Thermocomfort. He was a disaster in even thinking he could negotiate his way out of this morass as I knew you could not trust the Thermocomfort people. He bungled everything.

For over a year I was in limbo, trying to do my job as MD of Energycare while the SGB Group main board director gave me strict instructions not to contact Thermocomfort. Meanwhile, my subordinates at Energycare Limited, seeing the writing on the wall, had started to line themselves up to take over from me if things were resolved between Thermocomfort and the SGB Group.

I had nobody to talk to or confide in apart from Barbara, who understandably was also concerned about the no man's land we were both in. The only information Barbara and I were getting changed on a week by week basis: on some occasions I was told that a deal was being done and I was the sacrificial lamb and would have to go, as Thermocomfort would not work with me; then I would be told that the SGB Group would take over Thermocomfort and I would be expected to run it with a merged Energycare Limited. I was also told that the SGB Group had spent over £250,000 on legal fees seeking out legal opinions on the legality of the Thermocomfort agreement. It was a lot of money and a complete waste: the Thermocomfort agreement was watertight—I knew this as I had drawn it up. I was also told that there had been a threat by Thermocomfort to use its Shell connections to cut off the heating oil supplies to the SGB Group headquarters building to try and bring them to heel.

During the year that this unsatisfactory state of affairs continued, Barbara and I did not have a clue as to whether we were coming or going. For me, it was ruining my health to the point where my doctor signed me off sick. I was on tranquilisers, antidepressants and sleeping tablets and drinking more than I should. How Thermocomfort Limited and the SGB Group treated me was without doubt a major factor in the breakdown of our marriage. I wish I had reacted differently to the situation: I could have just signed Barbara and me into the local golf club and let these two behemoths fight it out. But I was young and in this respect less business savvy. Nonetheless I could see the writing on the wall—that at some stage, however it panned out, my business connections with Energycare Limited would come to an end. As well as this, I always had on my mind that I had given my word to Barbara's first husband Buzz that I would reciprocate his agreeing to let Barbara and me take Tripp to live in England. So on a trip to California in January 1983 we put down a $5,000 deposit on a luxury condominium in the exclusive district known as 1998 Broadway, 1406, Pacific Heights, San Francisco. We chose this location because it would be exactly half way between Buzz's home and the school Tripp would be attending, thus making access easier all round.

On our return to the UK, Barbara and I had lunch at a restaurant in Weston-super-Mare, on 14 February 1983, with the Midland Bank regional manager, Leslie Pearce. Mr Pearce agreed to wire that afternoon $156,000 as a down payment to the Crocker Mortgage Company in Walnut Creek, California, a subsidiary of Midland Bank. He requested that as a special client of Midland Bank we would be granted a $100,000 mortgage to complete the purchase of the condominium. Everything Mr Pearce did was done without my signing any papers and was based solely on my word that I would pay him back the $156,000 out of the money I was due to receive from the SGB Group in July that year. So with no credit history, no employment in the US, and in my case not even a Social Security number, the impossible was achieved: Barbara and I now owned a luxury condominium in Pacific Heights, which we immediately put out to rent with the real estate agent who had sold it to us.

Apart from that quick jaunt to the States, it was a wretched time. I would like to make it clear, though, that no present member of Thermocomfort Limited or any of the staff of SGB Group Plc, including Peter Cox Limited, had anything to do with the foregoing.

Eventually, after a miserable year, I was told that the SGB Group and Thermocomfort had resolved their issues and part of the deal was that I was to go. I received back the money I had originally invested in Energycare, in the July of 1983. Now cash rich, I used some of it to repay the Midland Bank the money lent to me for the down payment on the condominium.

It was at this point that, despite my many successful, if sometimes unorthodox, decisions, I made one business decision that has come to haunt me, and had I not made that decision my entire life would have been different and the subject matter of this book would not have existed.

Throughout my business career, which took me from nothing to a major player, involved in my success was Mr Pearce, the same regional manager of the Midland Bank in Weston-super-Mare who had trusted me sufficiently to provide the money for the down payment on the condominium. It was he who had also given me, earlier in my business career, the all-important bank reference which had enabled me to get the huge government contract that had really set my business on its feet, and who would often go to great risk, from his point of view, by extending my overdraft by huge amounts, unsecured, as the company grew. Without this man my business career would not have reached the heights it did, yet I did a shameful thing that I will always regret—I closed my accounts with Mr Pearce because I wanted the 'snob value' of having a bank account with the most exclusive bank in the world—the Queen's bankers, Coutts & Co.

I was now able to keep the promise I had made to Barbara's first husband. Having now severed my business connections in the UK, Barbara and I rented out our Bristol home for a year and on 1 September 1983, now with two sons, we all moved to San Francisco.

At one time I had had a dream of becoming a Member of Parliament. I had thought it would be good to show that you could come from nowhere and become rich decently and honestly, and I wanted to use my skills to benefit my fellow citizens. With our change of continents this was obviously not to be.

Because I would need something to occupy me when we first arrived in California, I decided to write a book. Although not a writer I had an ambition to write the biography of someone who was a hero to me—one of the most important past leaders of US television programming, Dick Powell. His career had gone from starring in Busby Berkeley musicals to playing Philip Marlowe in feature films, and other starring roles. He became a successful film and television producer and director in his own right. His remarkable career gave a break to such stars as Steve McQueen, David Janssen and a plethora of other stars. He made most of the biggest television hits in the 1950s and 60s, some of which are still in worldwide syndication today. This ambition too was not to be fulfilled.

# MARRIAGE SHOCK

## Chapter 6

Within days of moving to Pacific Heights I had the shock of my life. Barbara announced that our marriage was over. I was dumbstruck. I could not imagine what I had possibly done wrong and was totally unable to get my head around this turn of events. I had even thought our marriage sufficiently stable that I had had a vasectomy as a surprise present for Barbara before we departed from England.

Barbara moved out, taking Graham Jnr with her, and went to stay in a friend's vacant house in Sausalito. I roamed around like a caged lion, missing my son dreadfully and not knowing for the life of me what to do.

One day, while still in a state of utter disbelief, I received a phone call from Rosanne Parr-Cox, Buzz's second wife. She and Barbara's former best girlfriend, Cathy Chatham, asked to meet with me, and from them I discovered at firsthand why her husband had so readily given in to his son going to England and why our marriage had 'failed'. The two women were at great pains to make me understand why this was, and wanted me to recognise that it was *not* of my making. It seemed that Barbara had an objective, this being to deny her first husband access to their son Tripp, and all the while she lived in England with him, her objective had been achieved. I was just a means to an end.

From them I heard a litany of all the things Barbara had done to frustrate her first husband's access to their son, including dropping him off without notice at the yacht club of which they were members, at the start of a couples race, forcing them to pull out; dating men who were members of the same club and making sure they were seated next to Buzz and Rosanne at dinner parties; moving south of San Francisco so that Buzz would be driving against the heavily congested traffic when he went to pick up his child for access. When I asked Rosanne why her husband had consented to the child going to live in England, I was told, "Well, Graham, frankly we were glad to get rid of her and get on with our marriage."

They also told me about Barbara's background and what was the final crunch that ended her first marriage. She came from humble stock, but her looks, her vivacious personality and wit, enabled her to marry into a wealthy, well-established San Francisco family where she encountered a lifestyle she had not known before. However, she ran her husband ragged with the way she conducted herself in the marriage. The final straw came when, having invited his best friend and his wife to dinner, her husband arrived home to find a note on the dining room table addressed to him, stating simply that she had gone off north to Lake Thane and taken Tripp with her. Deciding enough was enough, Buzz moved out, rented a new home and started divorce proceedings. It was his good luck, and Barbara's misfortune, that the very first weekend he was away starting his new life he met Rosanne, who became his second wife.

Barbara now had a big problem, because suddenly she was faced with the fact that there was no going back to her husband. What she therefore did was to invite Buzz to dinner at the plush Alta Mira Hotel in Sausalito to discuss, so he thought, arrangements for their son. What he did not know was that Barbara had booked a room, with champagne at the ready, so that when, as she anticipated, he stayed the night with her, it would be the end of his relationship with Rosanne. When Buzz discovered this he left $500, a lot of money in those days, on the table as a gesture, and left.

Where this story gets awfully sinister is that when Barbara and I got married it was she who booked the room for the first night—the selfsame room in the selfsame hotel.

I too had seen a cruel streak in her I had not noticed in the early days. For example, after we were married we rented a home over the Christmas period at Lake Tahoe, California, and invited her parents to stay with us. At this time her father was suffering from senile dementia and no sooner had we got to Lake Tahoe than he wanted to go back to the senior citizens' centre he attended in Napa. This went on for almost a week with her father being harangued throughout the day by both Barbara and her mother.

One morning I awoke and her father was not there. I was stunned to find that Barbara and her mother had borrowed the next-door neighbour's four-by-four (better equipped for snow than our vehicle) and had put him on a Greyhound bus back to Napa. After his arrival back in Napa, for the next few days this old and mentally ill man tried to drive back up to Lake Tahoe. He kept being stopped by the California Highway Patrol due to the snow on the road, so he would then turn south and drive to Marin County to be with Barbara's brother, who would entertain him for a while and then let him leave to complete the cycle of going back to Napa, then Lake Tahoe.

In the end I put my foot down and declared that either Barbara's mother went back to Napa or I would, and in the end her mother went back to take care of the old man.

On 24 July 1982, my father died. Now married and living in Bristol, Barbara and I went to Charlbury for his funeral. Even though my father was an incredibly highly decorated war hero, he would never talk about the war unless I plied him with whisky and tried to extract the stories from him. When he died at the age of sixty-three from a heart attack, I came up with an idea to show him how much I loved him. The night before his funeral I went to the undertakers with a bottle of Bells whisky, two cut-glass whisky glasses and a film camera case with a note in it telling him how much I loved him and we would have a drink together one day, although hopefully a long time off. I got the undertaker to lift the coffin lid and I placed the bottle, glasses and camera case inside. I told no one of what I had done, except my mother. As he had always been very popular, at his funeral people lined the streets as the coffin was taken from the church to the cemetery, and you could hear the clinking of the glass inside. Thus in a grave in Charlbury, Oxfordshire, is a well-matured bottle of Bells.

Here it was that I had another glimpse of Barbara's unfeeling nature. As I stood by the graveside with tears rolling down my cheeks, to the shock of everyone who witnessed this, Barbara turned to me and all I heard her say was, "Grow up and be a man".

Then there was her intransigence that I could never fathom. She didn't work, and we had money rolling in, but she would not take her car to have a child seat fitted, so I had to do it. She didn't want to do housework—no problem there, I hired a cleaner to come in three times a week. After a few days the cleaner never reappeared, and when I asked Barbara I was told she did not like having the cleaner around while she was at home. The insurance company insisted we install a burglar alarm because of all the valuables we both had, and although she knew the insurance company would deny cover if the alarm was not on, she would *not* switch it on.

Barbara's intransigence had been a constant feature of our marriage, as illustrated yet again by the following. She had a largish trunk and in it were all her past photographs and memorabilia, a large portion of which related to her first wedding and marriage. She insisted that the trunk should sit in our bedroom closet in our Bristol home. When I objected to this and moved it to the storage room, she simply hauled it out and put it back in our bedroom closet. In the end I just gave up as it became a futile exercise.

There was one later incident that illustrates the obsession Barbara had with money. This took place when, attempting a reconciliation again, we were living in the condominium in San Francisco. One day I needed a small amount of cash and could not be bothered to go to the bank, so without telling Barbara, for the first and only time I took $20 from her purse. Later on in the day, after she returned from shopping, she checked what cash she had in her handbag and announced she was off to do some errands. When she returned she told me she had been to every store she had visited that day, including ones on the other side of Golden Gate Bridge (to reach which she would have had to pay the Golden Gate toll), to ask the stores to check their cash till balances.

In retrospect, and with the gift of hindsight, I should have seen all the warning background signs that something was amiss and that I was walking into a bizarre world. There was Barbara's first husband all too eagerly agreeing to his son moving overseas. Barbara's modus operandi in relation to Tripp's father was already apparent in that I would often walk into my study to find the phone off the receiver on the desk and Buzz on the other end waiting to talk to his son. What Barbara was doing was deliberately not telling Tripp that his father was on the phone.

I had Barbara's mother refusing to have a phone installed, so that while Barbara was living in Bristol with me and was able to call her mother in the States at any time and for as long as she liked, it never happened. I even went to the time and expense of getting a local US phone company to install a phone in her home, but the engineer was turned away at the door. Yet, as soon as the marriage failed and Barbara was living virtually on her mother's doorstep, her mother then had a phone put in.

There was another peculiar incident when I was invited to dinner at the exclusive St Francis Yacht Club with Cathy Chatham and her husband 'Davy Crockett' Chatham, who was a drunk. There were four of us supposedly having a pleasant dinner. A debacle then ensued that consisted of Davy Crocket Chatham wrestling my Rolex watch off my wrist in the packed restaurant so as to compare it with the weight of his own and check if mine was a fake. He then announced it was genuine.

If that was not bizarre enough, Barbara and I went to the wedding of one of her brother's son's, at Newport Beach in southern California. Nothing strange here except that as soon as the ceremony was over her brother literally disappeared as he was in hiding because of gambling debts and the enforcers were after him. Barbara was quite prepared to leave town without seeing him as he was on the run. I had to put my foot down here because it didn't seem right that she should abandon her brother when he needed support.

When divorce proceedings were started on 9 September 1983, at the San Francisco Superior Court, it stunned me to discover that for the duration of our marriage Barbara had been copying all the bank statements and requisite financial documents. In view of what was to come, this pointed to a fair degree of premeditation.

Her planning was immaculate as well as cunning. After declaring our marriage was over she went, as said, to live in nearby Sausalito. I was living on the monthly severance pay I was getting from the SGB Group, using it also to furnish the condominium and buy a car. As soon as she knew the severance money from SGB had come to an end, she applied to the court for a restraining order to get me out of the condominium. This was cruel: I had burned all my bridges and had literally nowhere to go because the Bristol home was rented out. I was forced to rent an apartment.

It came as an incredible shock to my system that suddenly, there I was in California, April 1984, living in a small flat, with no friends, no family, and equally as important, no knowledge of the Californian legal system. The long and the short of it was, I not only ended up in rented accommodation, I also ended up in a quandary: I had two daughters in England with an ex-wife determined to frustrate my contact with them, and an eighteen-month-old son who had been living with us in California. Tripp, meanwhile, had returned to live with his father, who had swiftly taken custody of him, not wanting to be dragged into access games with his ex-wife. Barbara had no option but to accept this as she could not fight me for Graham Jnr and for Tripp as well.

So not only had I problems with Jane and my daughters, I now had a second wife frustrating physical access to my children. Barbara had already attempted to thwart access to the father of her first son; it now looked likely she was going to repeat this behaviour with me and her second son. What a mess.

# THE DUPLICITY OF MY LAWYER,
## URIE WALSH

## Chapter 7

As lawyers go, Urie W. Walsh must surely rank as the lowest of the low. Had I hired a drunk from the Golden Gate Park in San Francisco to represent me, I would have been better off than hiring Urie Walsh. At least the drunk would not have had a California State Bar licence entitling him to practise law.

Needing a Californian lawyer to handle my divorce proceedings, I had phoned my mother in England and asked her if she could remember the name of the young Californian who was studying at Oxford and who had been dating the girl who was my mother's lodger at the time. I had met this lawyer once at a Christmas dinner at my mother's home some fifteen years earlier when I was nineteen, still doing my apprenticeship and trying in my spare time to get an old Vauxhall Victor back on the road. Michael Friedman was his name, and it was Michael Friedman who recommended me to the Californian lawyer, Urie Walsh—and Michael Friedman who appears again later in this story, in cahoots with that same lawyer.

I tracked Friedman down by phone and discovered that he lived and worked in Sausalito, which is just outside San Francisco. Michael Friedman told me he had a friend, Urie Walsh, who had handled some of his partners' and friends' divorces. So I phoned Urie Walsh and we arranged to meet at his law offices, Walsh and Cullen, 1111 Oak Street, San Francisco.

As agreed, I met Urie Walsh at 10am on a Sunday morning and he agreed to represent me, providing me with a Retainer Agreement along with a Deed of Trust and Promissory Note (the equivalent of a charge against the condominium as a guarantee for the payment of any fees). I had no idea at that time what a Deed of Trust or Promissory Note was.

He told me to look over the documents and come back to his office at 9am the next day, Monday morning. It was then that Urie Walsh committed a number of violations of the California Rules of Professional Conduct and state law. For one thing, he did not tell me to seek legal advice as he was required to do under the rules.

The Retainer Agreement that Urie Walsh violated:

*. . . As the Attorney and Client acknowledge in the Retainer Agreement that Client has an interest in the subject real property, it is the Committee's opinion that Attorney is obliged to comply with the requirements set forth in Rule 3-300(A), (B) and (C). Specifically, compliance requires the Attorney to ensure that:*

*(A) The transaction or acquisition and its terms are fair and reasonable to the client and are fully disclosed and transmitted in writing to the client in a manner which should reasonably have been understood by the client; and (B) The client is advised in writing that the client may seek the advice of an independent lawyer of the client's choice and is given a reasonable opportunity to seek that advice; and (C) The client thereafter consents in writing to the terms of the transaction or the terms of the acquisition.*

I should have smelt a rat as to the way he practised law as, shortly after I met him, I picked up a short-term driving ban for a motoring infraction. He told me it was only my Californian driver's licence that had been suspended so I could continue to drive on my international licence. I thought this advice was suspect and sure enough, when I checked with the California Highway Patrol, they informed me I could not drive on the roads in California while the ban was in place no matter how many licences I had.

About five months later, realising that things were not working out between Barbara and me, I requested a meeting with Urie Walsh. At the meeting I asked him to draw up a comprehensive marriage settlement agreement which would allow me to put things to rest so that I could move on, which he did. He signed the agreement, I signed the agreement and took it home for Barbara to sign. However, he had made a classic legal blunder. Barbara's lawyer, Gail Connolly had indicated in the past that she intended to withdraw as Barbara's Attorney of Record. The critical point here was that she had not withdrawn, but neither had she been consulted about the agreement, and without her signature the marriage settlement agreement was worse than worthless. I did not know this, and in fact Urie Walsh specifically told me that he would go to court and get the agreement enforced. At this point Barbara and I were both back in the condominium having attempting a reconciliation, which had failed.

In yet another classic blunder I was told by Urie Walsh to go back to the UK and start to perform my part of the financial side of the agreement, which of course meant reorganising all my financial affairs and taking on substantial financial liabilities. According to Urie Walsh, this would be seen by the court as my acting 'in good faith'. In point of fact his instruction had nothing to do with good faith. He simply wanted me out of the way as he knew that the court would quite rightly throw out the first marriage settlement agreement as it was invalid, Barbara's lawyer not having signed it. Of course at the time I did not know this and trusted his advice, all of which made his actions the more reprehensible as he knew I would be getting deeper into debt with Coutts & Co. As if this was not enough, he was charging me for this charade and later sued me for his fees for this mess of his own making.

It is probably accurate to write that there is not a family lawyer in California who would have given me the advice or instruction to vacate the condominium and leave California before the court had ratified the marriage settlement agreement.

In the meantime Barbara's lawyer, Gail Connolly, had filed an application with the court to set the agreement to one side. Both Urie Walsh and Gail Connolly were underwriting their fees via Deeds of Trust against the condominium in Pacific Heights, both of which were obtained in direct violation of the California Rules of Professional Conduct.

When I returned to England, I quickly arranged a meeting with my bankers Coutts & Co. for 19 October 1984, in Bristol. During the course of the meeting I produced the first marriage settlement agreement that Urie Walsh had told me, orally and in writing, would be upheld and ratified by the court. Then I did exactly as Urie Walsh told me to do, which was to arrange for the bank to make two payments. One was to mail to Urie Walsh a cashier's cheque to pay his outstanding legal fees, and the second was to send him a cashier's cheque to pay three months' mortgage payments on the condominium in San Francisco. Both transactions were carried out on the same day that I met with Coutts & Co.

The ensuing mistake made by Coutts & Co. would have been of no consequence had it not been for the subsequent actions of Urie Walsh. They inadvertently sent the envelope to Urie Walsh at 11 Oak Street, San Francisco, when in fact it should have gone to 1111 Oak Street. This was a simple human error and was rectified by the bank, after oral communications with Urie Walsh's secretary, by means of a Coutts & Co. direct wire transfer to his bank account in San Francisco for the full amount of both cashier's cheques. There is no doubt he received these as he paid the three months' mortgage payments.

Urie Walsh had told me that he would go to court and rigorously defend the marriage settlement agreement. I found out later that this was a lie as he knew—but I didn't—that with Barbara's lawyer as Attorney of Record there was no court in California that would have enforced this marriage settlement agreement and there would never have been a hearing. Of course at this juncture I had an overdraft, had reorganised my affairs and was living in Bristol thinking I had put San Francisco and California behind me. But after the failure of this first marriage settlement agreement, I had no choice but to return to San Francisco to sort out all the problems I thought it had resolved, and initiate through my lawyer a second agreement. Of course by now I was in a worse position as I had not only started a new business in England but I had also reorganised all of my personal finances with Coutts & Co. This included paying off the mortgage arrears on the condominium in San Francisco to the Crocker Mortgage Company, paying off our joint overdraft, and paying Urie Walsh his outstanding fees.

Another problem I had was the hugely valuable block of UK stock-exchange-listed shares owned by me, held on deposit at Shearson Lehman American Express, San Francisco, which Coutts & Co. wanted back in the United Kingdom as security for their financing the first marriage settlement. These shares were the subject of a restraining order, keeping them in California, a fact well known to Urie Walsh as he was my lawyer when the restraining order was put into effect. While those shares were stuck in San Francisco they were of no benefit to me or, as importantly, to Coutts & Co. Indeed, as time dragged on, the value of those shares was declining and Coutts & Co. could only take my word they even existed.

# URIE WALSH AND THE SECOND MARRIAGE
# SETTLEMENT AGREEMENT

## Chapter 8

A t this juncture it is to be noted that I still believed what Urie Walsh had told me, that the first marriage settlement agreement had been set aside because Barbara was claiming she had been coerced, when in fact there had never even been a hearing. Contrary to what Urie Walsh had told me, there was never any chance the first marriage settlement agreement would stand up in court as it had not been signed by Barbara's lawyer. As I was to find out later, Urie Walsh was guilty of legal malpractice at this juncture, but knowing no better I believed his false story that the failure of the first marriage settlement agreement was my fault—after all, I came from a culture where you believed in the integrity of your lawyer. Inevitably, Urie Walsh charged me for his bungling.

On my return to San Francisco, our attempted reconciliation having failed, on Urie Walsh's direct advice I got a locksmith to let me in and entered the condominium. Urie Walsh meanwhile phoned Barbara's lawyer, Gail Connolly, to tell her I was back in California and back in the condominium. She immediately applied to the San Francisco Superior Court for a restraining order to get me out, which Judge Isabella Horton Grant flatly refused to do, pointing out that a) Christmas was coming, and b) I had returned specifically to sort things out, and having me holed up in a hotel would not speed up any resolution of the situation. Also, Barbara had family and friends in or around San Francisco with whom she could stay.

We were all ordered to go away and come back the next day with settlement proposals. Accordingly, we met at Urie Walsh's office and the pressure was on me. I had not seen my son for some time and it was nearly Christmas. I had re-established myself in business in the United Kingdom and needed to get back, not least because my twin daughters needed their father to be with them in the UK, not getting dragged into legal quicksand in California. Coutts & Co. were unhappy because they had not seen the promised funds or share certificates which were languishing in San Francisco. Urie Walsh was claiming that his partner was complaining about his bill even though he had just been paid $5,000 (later the partner denied this) and he had succeeded in convincing me that the failure of the first marriage settlement agreement was my fault.

A new marriage settlement/reconciliation agreement was drawn up by Urie Walsh and presented to Barbara and her lawyer Gail Connolly. Later, in the malpractice action, experts would state it was impossible to determine exactly what type of agreement this was (whether it was a settlement or reconciliation agreement), and that they thought that what Urie Walsh was actually up to was to get in place a new agreement to try and get himself off the hook in regards to the failure of the first one.

I was concerned about what was in this new agreement, the critical point being there was absolutely no reference to my son or what would happen as to custody or access in the event that the reconciliation failed. Simply put, I would be paying vast sums of money to Barbara with nothing in return if the marriage failed. I asked Urie Walsh for time to think things through. At this juncture he did something that stunned me: he jumped up, called Barbara and her lawyer into his office and insisted over and over again that unless I agreed to the terms and conditions he would withdraw as my lawyer there and then. As stated, I was stunned. I had never had a lawyer treat me in such a demeaning way. However, when I then requested it, Urie Walsh gave me his solemn undertaking that he would remain my lawyer while the ramifications of the agreement were being worked through. Barbara and I left Urie Walsh's office and went back to the condominium together; I at least was hoping for another reconciliation.

After being forced into agreeing to the second marriage

settlement by Urie Walsh, the time came the next day when we would all have to go before Judge Grant and have the agreement entered into the court record so that it would become enforceable. On the morning of the hearing, coming upon Urie Walsh in the corridor of the San Francisco Superior Court outside Judge Grant's chambers, I again told him that I was unhappy with the agreement which committed me to so much and Barbara to so little. Thereupon, Urie Walsh again called Gail Connolly over and reiterated that if I did not agree to have the agreement entered into the court record he was walking out. With Christmas coming and wanting to spend time with my son, I had no choice but to have the second marriage settlement agreement, which I believed was a reconciliation agreement, read in court.

As part of the agreement, the Dodge Omni car (registration 1 GPL 700, I remember it well), which I had purchased while separated from Barbara, had fractionally under $5,000 owing on it. I was expected to pay this off, but as Barbara would get the use of the car I was very reluctant to concede to this arrangement. What Urie Walsh did was to tell me that if I signed the second marriage settlement agreement he would knock the money owed on the Dodge Omni off my bill, remain as my Attorney of Record while the provisions of the second marriage agreement were being implemented and, just as importantly, apply to get the restraining order taken off the block of shares held at Shearson Lehman American Express. I could then get them back to Coutts & Co. in England to whom they had originally been promised. I agreed.

After having had the second marriage agreement ratified by the court, both Barbara and I had to decide what to do over the forthcoming Christmas period. Barbara had previously planned that her father and mother would come to stay at the condominium on Christmas Eve, and on Christmas Day they would travel with Graham Jnr to Barbara's brother's home in Marin County for her parents to spend the day there. As the situation between Barbara and me was still delicate and her parents were very elderly, I offered to check into a local hotel and spend Christmas morning helping serve Christmas dinners at the local Salvation Army Hostel, returning at noon to the condominium. Barbara had promised she would return from her brother's after lunch so I could spend the rest of the day with her and Graham Jnr.

Time went by and there was no Barbara, let alone our son. Then Barbara returned to the condominium—without him. I was stunned to find out that the only reason she had returned was to take delivery of her first son, Tripp, from his father's home and return with him to her brother's in Marin County. I was horrified; the second marriage agreement was only a few days old and Barbara was already riding a coach and horses through it. There was nothing I could do and I did not get to see my son until late in the evening when she returned after picking up Tripp from her brother's and then dropping him off at his father's. All in all she had messed everyone around.

On Boxing Day it had already been arranged that Barbara would go over to Buzz's home and pick up Tripp for the day, and I went with her. When we arrived, Tripp, who I had not seen for fifteen months, ran to me and jumped into my arms, to be told by Barbara, "Never do that again." However there was one glimmer of decency when Buzz came up to me, shook my hand and told me, "Graham, I cannot thank you enough for what you have done for my son".

That same day I tried to get hold of Urie Walsh to tell him what had happened but he refused to take my phone calls. In fact I called him constantly before I subsequently had to leave for England, all to no avail.

On the very first business day after Christmas I was shocked to receive from Urie Walsh a Notice of Withdrawal of Attorney of Record, which of course was a direct violation of the undertaking he had given me at the time of inducing me to enter into the second marriage settlement agreement. This way he caused me yet another problem. I had contacted Shearson Lehman American Express, who had told me that as the shares they were holding were subject to a restraining order they would need a new court order to release them to me; either that or I would have to wait until the restraining order expired. I would need a lawyer—i.e. Urie Walsh, as I did not have the money to hire another one—to get the restraining order taken off, and I had businesses to run in the UK, so I had no choice but to get my designated return flight to England, leaving Barbara to bring our son along later. My hope was that we could resume our home life in Bristol and attempt another reconciliation.

After three months Barbara finally came to England with Graham Jnr on 1 April 1985, but it took some nudging. I had already told her emphatically there would be no more financial payments until my son was back in England. What I did not know was what her plan really entailed, which was to exploit a provision in Californian matrimonial law wherein either party could after six months vacate—pull out of—a settlement agreement if one party was induced to enter into the agreement by fraud or duplicity. So Barbara had to keep me sweet for six months.

No sooner had she arrived in England with Graham Jnr than she had to return to California because her father had died, and while she was in California our son, who was now approaching three years old, stayed with me in Bristol. By the time she returned to England after her father's funeral, she had dragged out four of the six months before I realised what she was really up to. I still did not know about the envelope from Coutts & Co. that had got lost in the mail, or, critically, as I was to find out much later, that all along Barbara had a rented home to go to in Napa, California. What she had done was rented out the condominium in San Francisco, put the furniture in storage, quit her job, and brought Graham Jnr to England: she had even enrolled him in preschool and bought the school uniform while knowing all along what she intended to do.

As it transpired, it did not take much nudging as Urie Walsh had made yet another massively incompetent blunder. Previously, writing through her lawyer, Barbara had waived any claim she had on 'the English properties' which of course included my Bristol home. Walsh failed to confirm this in the second marriage agreement. We discovered later that one of the many clandestine things Barbara did upon her return to England was to engage the services of a Bristol solicitor to see what she would need to do in England to make a claim against this property. I paid a very high price for Urie Walsh's legal negligence and his subsequent refusal to return my files, although required to do so by The State Bar of California Rules of Professional Conduct.

It is important to remember that by this time I was only too aware of the pathological ends Barbara had gone to in her efforts to deny her first husband access to their son, and in the year I had spent in limbo in California I experienced for myself what she did to frustrate my access to our son. My plan was therefore, at whatever cost to me personally or financially, to placate Barbara, simply so that I could have my three children around me, which of course included Ann and Louise. To this end I started a small commercial travel agency so that not only would it give Barbara an interest but also meant she could travel cheaply and freely back and forth to California to see Tripp and her widowed mother. As well as this, so that she would have her own space, I also put down a deposit on a luxury new flat in Battersea, London, which she subsequently arranged to be decorated; it was a case of literally anything to keep her happy and in England.

Barbara and our son's presence in Bristol strengthened my position with my first wife Jane, and I was able to force her hand and permit Ann and Louise to come and visit—the first time I had seen them in nearly eighteen months.

# URIE WALSH HAD HIS OWN AGENDA

## Chapter 9

As I have said, when Coutts & Co. realised they had mailed the envelope to Urie Walsh to 11 Oak Street, San Francisco, instead of 1111 Oak Street, both over the telephone and in writing they arranged with Urie Walsh to put a stop on the two cashier's cheques and to wire the money directly into his bank account, which was done. However, nobody could have predicted what Urie Walsh (who by his own admission was going through a partnership split and suffering from a cash flow problem) would do with the cheques when they eventually turned up on 21 January 1985. He knew the envelope had been mailed with the wrong address on it and had gone astray, and when it finally turned up it had to be obvious that the cheques in that envelope were the same ones he knew had been stopped, especially as they and the accompanying letter were dated three months before.

However, what he did was to deposit the cashier's cheque of $5,000 that was made out to him, into his account, and go off on vacation, drawing cheques against the $5,000. In the subsequent malpractice action against him, he was never able to explain why he did not forward to the Crocker Mortgage Company their cheque, which was one of the two in the envelope. Simple logic would dictate that if he thought the cheque to him was good, then he would have forwarded the mortgage company their cheque too, especially as on the very same date that the lost envelope turned up in his mail, a letter from them also arrived, asking for funds, as the mortgage was again three months in arrears. Obviously, the cheque was for the exact amount.

When Urie Walsh returned from vacation he discovered that some of his trust account cheques had bounced, and to cover his tracks he came up with a plan which he told to all and sundry. He told everyone *I had bounced a cheque on him*, and not satisfied with this, even blasted a letter off to the manager of the Coutts and Co. branch in England that held my account, the purpose being that he could copy the letter to other people to cover his tracks. But he *never* copied the letter to me. I was in total ignorance of all this. My relationship with Coutts & Co. was already strained due to my not being able to produce on the first marriage settlement agreement, and due also to the consequences of the second marriage settlement agreement.

In response to Urie Walsh's letter to them, Coutts & Co. wrote back a detailed letter confirming what had been agreed with him, namely that a stop had been put on the two cashier's cheques and that the replacement funds had been wired to his bankers. They also cryptically asked, if he had received the stopped cashier's cheque that was made payable to him, where was the cashier's cheque to the mortgage company which was in the same envelope? This letter to Urie Walsh came into my possession when, very much later in the story, I discovered his false claim that I had bounced a cheque on him, at which point I requested that Coutts & Co. let me know what on earth Urie Walsh was alleging.

Coutts & Co. is the most exclusive bank in the world. To bank with them is one of the privileges of wealth, and their bank managers are left with a great deal of discretion when dealing with their clients. Urie Walsh's conduct ended up ruining my relationship with them and destroying my position of privilege.

I was by this time trying to build up my new businesses in the UK. However, I had problems: Urie Walsh had withdrawn as my Attorney of Record, against my wishes and in direct contradiction of the undertaking he had given me, and I still did not have the block of shares on deposit with Shearson Lehman American Express in San Francisco, the block of shares I had promised Coutts & Co. to part-fund the failed first marriage settlement agreement, not to mention the second marriage settlement agreement.

All this was well known to Urie Walsh as he had promised,

when inducing me to sign the second marriage settlement agreement, to get the San Francisco Superior Court's restraining order on the block of shares lifted. Coutts & Co. were, understandably, not happy. Apart from the fact they had seen no money or security for the payments they had made, in defence of Coutts & Co. they had no proof these share certificates even existed and they were furious that Barbara was back in England because they thought the first marriage settlement agreement had settled all the issues. Throughout this entire time Urie Walsh had refused to take my numerous phone calls and had totally failed to respond to any of my written communications.

Instead he decided to sue me.

At this point I had one statement from him showing a $5,000 deduction of what he alleged I owed (in fact I did not owe even the net figure). When I got this statement I assumed he had done what he had given me an undertaking to do, which was deduct the amount owed on the finance agreement for the Dodge Omni car, which at the date of the second marriage settlement agreement was a couple of dollars short of $5,000. Of course at this time I knew nothing about the original problems caused by the Coutts & Co. envelope containing the cashier's cheques going to the wrong address, let alone what Urie Walsh had done with them when they subsequently turned up at his office. I was completely in the dark over all of this.

I received another statement from Urie Walsh, this time adding back the $5,000. This set me off on yet more attempts to contact him, trying to find out what was going on. These difficulties were compounded by the fact that I was seven thousand miles away in the UK and dealing with an eight-hour time difference. It was not even as if Urie Walsh was at any financial risk as he was holding a Promissory Note secured by the Deed of Trust against the condominium in San Francisco, guaranteeing he would get paid, come what may. He sued me in England for his concept of the full amount of the alleged fees owing, while totally failing to comply with the mandatory requirements of the Business and Professions Code 6201(a) which reads, in part:

> . . . *an attorney shall forward a written notice to the client prior to or at the time of service of summons or claim in an action against the client, or prior to*

*or at the commencement of any other proceeding against the client under a contract between attorney and client which provides for an alternative to arbitration under this article, for recovery of fees, costs, or both.*

Had I known this, one phone call to the State Bar of California requesting fee arbitration would have stopped Urie Walsh in his tracks, a fact that, as a practising lawyer, he must have been aware of, as the Business and Professions Code 6201(b) reads as follows:

*If an attorney, or the attorney's assignee, commences an action in any court or any other proceeding and the client is entitled to maintain arbitration under this article, and the dispute is not one to which subdivision (B) of Section 6200 applies, the client may stay the action or other proceeding by serving and filing a request for arbitration in accordance with the rules established by the board of trustees pursuant to subdivision (A) of Section 6200. The request for arbitration shall be served and filed prior to the filing of an answer in the action or equivalent response in the other proceeding; failure to so request arbitration prior to the filing of an answer or equivalent response shall be deemed a waiver of the client's right to arbitration under the provisions of this article if notice of client's rights to arbitration was given pursuant to subdivision (B).*

Urie Walsh knew the law, but as for me, having never been a long-time resident of California, I had no inkling of the mandatory fee arbitration process or who to turn to for help.

Walsh's activities did not stop there; he served his lawsuit for his alleged outstanding fees by mail, using the lowest possible response timescales permitted under California law—five days when they were served by mail and a further five days when they were served out of state. In fact he mailed the papers to my mother's address, knowing I wasn't living there. My mother was away so her neighbour signed for the envelope containing Urie Walsh's lawsuit, and when my mother returned she forwarded it to me, all of which necessarily wasted valuable time.

He had yet another trump card up his sleeve: there were no judicial response papers, as required by law, amongst the papers in the envelope. Consequently, I had to call the clerk of the San Francisco Municipal Court, who promised to mail me the required papers.

These I never received because, the hand of fate showing up yet again, the clerk forgot to put 'England' on the envelope, and when the mistake was subsequently discovered, the envelope containing the response papers was returned by the US mail to the clerk. As a consequence Urie Walsh requested that the court enter a default judgment against me: i.e. I had lost.

Even if I had been living in California it would have been difficult to keep up with the speed with which Urie Walsh was acting against me. And all the time, in suing me the way he did, he violated the California Rules of Professional Conduct and California Court Rules and Procedures. He also committed perhaps the most flagrant abuse of all my rights, whereby his whole method of suing me in England the way he did, was in express violation of a treaty signed by both the United States and the United Kingdom: The Hague Convention on the Service Abroad of Judicial and Extrajudicial Documents in Civil or Commercial Matters. Was it unreasonable to have expected the then Municipal Court judge, David Garcia, to have spotted my (the defendant's) UK address and asked or insisted that the protections of the Hague Convention be put in place?

Having obtained his default judgment, Urie Walsh then filed an application with the courts to order that the condominium in San Francisco be put up for a sheriff's sale—a public property auction, the last step in the foreclosure process after defaulting on a mortgage—to satisfy his judgment against me. There was nothing I could do. I still did not have the block of shares from San Francisco as I couldn't get Urie Walsh to even respond, let alone explain what he was doing, or to explain why he was claiming money I knew I did not owe him.

It later transpired that Barbara had made phone calls to Urie Walsh from England to try and find out what was going on and he refused to take her phone calls too, citing attorney-client conflict. This of course was utter bunkum as Urie Walsh had ceased to be my lawyer and, as he was well aware, Gail Connolly had also ceased to be Barbara's lawyer. In fact, as a judgment creditor holding a Deed of Trust on the condominium she jointly owned with me, with a sheriff's sale looming, Urie Walsh had a duty to talk to her.

# THE ABDUCTION

## Chapter 10

To pull off what she intended to do, Barbara would need help, and to this end she found a perfect accomplice. I was having problems with one of my main business colleagues whose wife had recently died and who felt he simply could not cope with the stress of being in business. The main propellant to curtailing our business relationship was Barbara constantly quoting her mantra, "If he can't shape up he needs to ship out", so my colleague and I parted company. As the parting seemed to be amicable I thought that was the end of the matter.

On the Friday night before the abduction on 1 July 1985, Barbara said she was going out for a drink with a girlfriend and I thought no more about it. She did not return that night and the next morning she phoned to say she had had too much to drink and had fallen asleep on the couch. She asked if we could meet for lunch at the Holiday Inn in Bristol, which we did. She repeated her story about not returning home because she was over the drink-driving limit and added that she did not phone because she had not woken up until the following morning. I accepted her explanation and we had a very pleasant lunch with her wearing the latest dress I had bought her. She even told me how happy she was that the marriage had been saved. And so I spent a very normal day—the day of the abduction— with Barbara and our son, shopping in the town of Bath.

Urie Walsh's activities were still going on in the background and I thought that I would soon go back to California and have it out with him. We returned home at about 4pm and I went to my office. There had been no rows or upsets and everything seemed as usual. When I returned home around 7pm the house was empty and I thought Barbara had taken Graham Jnr to the nearby park. I went there, couldn't see them and returned home. I asked the caretakers of our building if they had seen Barbara and Graham Jnr and was surprised to be told that a man in a car had picked them up.

Now panic set in. Both the car and the man fitted the description of the former business colleague of mine, the same person Barbara was so keen I sever my business connections with. I immediately jumped to the conclusion Barbara had left me for him. That she was going back to California with our son did not occur to me until I realised the safe was open and that Barbara had taken everything of value she could carry, plus my green card without which I had no right of entry to the United States.

It was then that Barbara's history of taking off with her children really struck home. She had done it in her first marriage and already twice to me. The first time was when we were on vacation in the British Virgin Islands and she didn't like it because it was too hot and there were too many non-whites and too many mosquitoes. The second time was the year before when we were camping; she got fed up and just took off, leaving me stranded without a car.

Once I realised Barbara's intention I contacted the local police, who came to my home. I was shocked to discover that both Barbara and our son had caught the 17:15 flight from Bristol to the Republic of Ireland with an onward-bound flight to New York, although the latter plane they never actually boarded. The Bristol police were aware of this as, having checked in their bags with the New York airline but not boarded, the counter terrorism police in the Republic of Ireland had ordered the plane to circle Shannon Airport while the Bristol police checked out who Barbara was. However, there was nothing the Bristol police could do to get my son back as they were now outside their jurisdiction and she had not broken any UK law. So, with her declaration of being happy in our marriage still ringing in my ears, in the background of my mind I recalled how Barbara had a history of taking off with her child without the father's knowledge and consent and how it finally finished her first marriage. I came then to the inevitable conclusion this was happening again and, if not stopped, my son would be gone for good.

After the police had left I made two critical phone calls. The first was to my lawyer in London, Charles Doughty, a senior partner in one of London's premier law firms who also specialised in family law. He advised me to be at his office at 10am the next day and he would seek a High Court Order giving me temporary custody of my son, which I could take to the Republic of Ireland and request that the High Courts in Dublin uphold the English Order. I had no problems with this as our second marriage agreement was predicated on the fact that my son would be in the United Kingdom.

My second phone call was to a well-known ex-Scotland Yard policeman, now a private detective who specialised in travelling the world recovering abducted children. This was the same man I had previously hired to run background checks on my daughters' potential stepfather. After I had explained the situation he promised to call me back that night when he had any information as to where in Ireland my son was. I knew Barbara had a very good friend who lived in the Irish Republic although I did not know where. When this detective called back I was told that both Barbara and Graham Jnr had been tracked down to Barbara's friend's home in Coachford, County Cork. His fee was £10,000 to get my son back. Alarm bells rang when he added that because of where my son was he would have to take a team and they would have to be armed. When I phoned Charles Doughty I was told in no uncertain terms that both he and his law firm would have nothing to do with me if I attempted to go along with this plan, so that was the end of that.

The next day I travelled to London to meet with Charles Doughty and the barrister who would be representing me in the High Court in Dublin. Here I was to make one of many mistakes which in retrospect I would not have made again. Charles Doughty recommended that while we were in court I could also get an order awarding my Bristol home to me. I refused to do this because I was still not totally certain what Barbara's long-term intentions were: was this really the end of our marriage or had Barbara panicked and fled back to California to stop Urie Walsh forcing the sale of the condominium?

That afternoon I travelled from London to Dublin where I was met at the airport by the Dublin solicitors who had been instructed by Charles Doughty. The next day we appeared before a High Court Judge in Dublin who upheld my English custody order and not only ordered the immediate return of my son but also that all air and seaports be alerted as Graham Jnr was not to leave the Republic of Ireland. Armed with this Irish court order the court's bailiff travelled to Cork to serve the order on Barbara. When he knocked on the door the owner of the house brandished a shotgun, whereupon the bailiff withdrew and contacted the local police, the Garda. After a long while the Garda finally arrived and made a second attempt to serve the order, but by then the house was deserted, and that was it. We could only report to the High Court in Dublin the next day that my son could not be found. Somehow Barbara had managed to slip the net and travel with him to New York, and then on to San Francisco. To this day I have never been able to find out how she was able to get out of Ireland.

As there was no more I could do in Ireland I returned to my home in Bristol. I was devastated.

# AFTER THE ABDUCTION

## Chapter 11

At this juncture not only was I in total shock as a result of the abduction, I was well and truly boxed in without a clue of what to do next. I had no travel documents to enter the United States so as to try and resolve things there, and of course I could not manage any of the court appearances which I knew Barbara, Gail Connolly (who was now once again representing Barbara) and Urie Walsh were making. Coutts & Co. had been made aware of the abduction but they still had not received the share certificates they had been promised to cover the money they had advanced to fund the first marriage settlement agreement, and even were they to arrive they were plummeting in value due to market forces.

I had no idea the condominium was at risk as we had a tenant paying almost twice the cost of the mortgage payment and there was a rising property market; I was at this point unaware of Urie Walsh's background activities.

I had tried to see my daughters and was told by Jane that if I appeared to collect them she would call the police; there was no point in going to court in Bristol over this as I was already fighting on too many battlefronts. I had also to contend with the utter betrayal of the business partner whom I had known for years (although, as said, we had parted company at this point) who had aided and abetted Barbara by helping the pair get to the airport. As if that was not enough, he had withdrawn his guarantee to Coutts & Co. for the company's overdrafts, leaving me to pick up all the liability. Of course my remaining business partner and I tried as best we could to keep going, but my heart was not in it. I knew that once I retrieved my travel documents I would have no option but to go back to California.

I had also to contend with the nightmare of staying in my Bristol home with all its memories, not least of which was my son's bedroom which still had his tricycle there exactly as he had left it. For what turned out to be three months, I was living in limbo with things imploding around me in California, and Barbara, Gail Connolly and Urie Walsh running rampant, getting one order after another.

By now I was an emotional wreck, powerless to control events: whichever choice I took I would lose out. If I stayed in England and saved my businesses and enforced my rights to see my daughters, I would lose everything in California including access to my son. If I went to California everything in the UK would fall apart. For three months I lived in an alcoholic haze, lying on my bed drinking and filling myself with tranquillisers and antidepressants. Then a friend said to me very bluntly at this juncture, that if I carried on as I was *I would have nothing left*. This gave me the fillip I needed to get my act together.

I enlisted the help of a San Francisco lawyer named Albert Kun, who not only achieved the return of my travel documents but also managed to secure court-ordered telephone access at 1pm California time Mondays, Wednesdays and Fridays. Happy as I was about this, on each and every occasion the phone would be answered but left hanging, and every so often someone would come and bounce the phone against the wall, while all the time I could hear my son in the background. This practice not only created mental anguish for me but also racked up my phone bill.

On 1 October 1985, having organised my affairs as best I could in the United Kingdom, I travelled to San Francisco and from there to Napa, California, which I figured was the best place to start to find my son and Barbara, as her mother lived there. By this time I had not seen either of them for over three months. I checked into the Holiday Inn and went to the payphone thinking that I could ask Barbara's mother if she would help. What I discovered shook me, because listed in the telephone directory was Barbara's name, and I was in for another shock when, checking with the phone operator, I discovered that the entries for the Napa phone book had closed on 9

January that year. This meant that Barbara had rented the home she intended to move into before she had even brought our son to England, and she had done so within days of signing the second marriage settlement agreement. Nonetheless I phoned Barbara, who agreed that if we met the next day at the Embassy Suites Hotel in Napa we could discuss all the outstanding issues and I promised I would then leave California immediately. Naturally, she did not turn up. I think she took pleasure in the fact that I would be left dangling for months, or, as it turned out, for years.

I had other problems to deal with, such as all the court orders that had been made in California while I was stuck in England because my travel documents had been stolen. The court was well aware of the theft as it was Judge Horton Grant of the San Francisco Superior Court who had ordered these documents to be returned to me. In my absence, Barbara and Gail Connolly had obtained an order in the San Francisco Superior Court stopping Urie Walsh from forcing the sale of the condominium in the lower court, i.e. the San Francisco Municipal Court. In response, Urie Walsh had come back into the San Francisco Superior Court divorce proceedings to get that order vacated—overturned—and was successful. As everything he had done was both unethical and in violation of the California Rules of Professional Conduct, Judge Grant, as a judge of the Superior Court, had the power to look into Urie Walsh's underlying conduct in obtaining the San Francisco Municipal Court order to sell the condominium and rule it as void. Better still she could have reported him to the State Bar of California: on the contrary she showed no initiative and did nothing.

Barbara had already cleared out our joint funds at the Pacific Bank, San Francisco. With the help of her brother she had also removed from storage our furniture and all my personal possessions, which included my precious record collection that had taken years to build up. I never saw any of them again. Now another order was being made behind my back—it became obvious later that Barbara was panicking because Urie Walsh was bearing down on her with his proceedings for a sheriff's sale—so she obtained an order giving her permission to list the condominium for sale on the open market, and instructing the tenant to divert the rent cheques to her.

After I had settled into my hotel I travelled to the San Francisco Superior Court and filed an application for permission to see my son. To my surprise, on the day of the hearing, Barbara and her lawyer turned up, and to my consternation I discovered that the hearing was in fact all about selling the condominium. I did not know the condominium had been listed for sale—this was the first I had heard about it. The purchaser had already signed the sale contract but as co-owner it required my signature too. Without my signature the proposed purchaser could not get a mortgage as there would be in legal terms no clear title to the condominium.

Amongst others who turned up was the lawyer who represented 'the purchasers' of the condominium, the lawyer for the tenant of the condominium and, centre of attention, none other than Urie Walsh himself. Urie Walsh's appearance was particularly galling as, if he had responded to my requests for information about what was going on, and, more particularly, if he had behaved ethically, none of this would be happening. The real estate agent who had originally sold me the condominium was there too, this time to justify why the condominium had been sold, in a rapidly rising property market, at much less than I paid for it.

I was shocked to the core. Not only was the condominium gone, I had a whole army of lawyers lined up against me on what I thought was the simple matter of getting permission to see my son.

My proposal was to offer to pay off Urie Walsh's judgment and list the property for sale at its true market value. The court rejected this offer and I, furious by now, refused to sign the sale documents. As a result, the judge ordered three things. One was that her clerk could sign the sale documents, two was that I get a lawyer, and three, I could see my son but, for as long as my English and Irish custody orders (where I had been granted sole custody) remained in existence, only under supervision.

It is to be noted that having created this nightmare by obtaining his Municipal Court judgment and requesting a further order from the court for a sheriff's sale, for unknown reasons Urie Walsh backed off, and afterwards it was Barbara who drove the condominium into foreclosure by taking the rent cheques but not paying the mortgage. Nobody had thought things through and my offer to pay off Urie Walsh's disputed judgment and the mortgage arrears was the best option on the table. As regards my access, the original point of the hearing, I had walked into a maelstrom. Only weeks earlier the same San Francisco Superior Court judge, Judge Grant, had awarded weekend access to a Norwegian father who, on the first weekend had abducted his son back to Norway using a false seaman's pass and duplicate passports. Barbara was alleging, with no basis of fact, that I intended to abduct our son back to England. Of course I had no such plans and it had never even crossed my mind. The outcome was that I was ordered by the court to surrender my British passport and instructed not to apply for a new one for my son. This came with a specific promise by Judge Grant—which she subsequently broke— that I could have my passport back from the court if and when I requested it.

It was after this first hearing that, in the corridors of the courthouse, Barbara made the following statement: "If you had not bounced a cheque on your lawyer none of this would have happened", which was *the first I ever knew* about anything to do with the cashier's cheques to Urie Walsh. The next day I phoned Coutts & Co. in Bristol and began to unravel Walsh's lies over what had happened.

As ordered, the next day I hired a lawyer. His name was Joel Belway Esq., a partner in a new law firm, Belway, Lombard and Carrington. (One of these partners was later disbarred on an unrelated matter.) I paid him a $5,000 retainer to represent me in the child custody matter and resolve the issues resulting from Urie Walsh's conduct and the sale of the condominium. However, although he was a pleasant young man he was inexperienced, and it transpired that he went about everything in exactly the wrong way. He filed Notice of Appeals against the court orders made by Judge Grant relating to the sale of the condominium, which only served to antagonise her; this was doubly unfortunate as she happened to be the judge who was also handling my custody hearing. What Joel Belway should have done was to file an application with the San Francisco Municipal

Court, a subordinate court, so as to vacate all of Urie Walsh's orders on the basis they were obtained by fraud; by violation of the California Rules of Professional Conduct; by violation of Californian law; and by violation of The Hague Convention on the Service Abroad of Judicial and Extrajudicial Documents in Civil or Commercial Matters.

The list of Joel Belway's mishandlings is almost endless, including the fact that any application to the court to set aside the Urie Walsh judgment at that time was not time-barred so there was no statute of limitation problem, meaning we were within the six months mandated by law for setting aside the judgment. The tactic he should have used was to order up the San Francisco Municipal Court file and put me in contact with a legal malpractice lawyer. Had this been done, we could have proceeded to bring a legal malpractice action against Urie Walsh there and then, with the result that the condominium need not have been sold and all the heat and anger that permeated the underlying custody action would have subsided. A major factor here was simply the cultural one. It was unheard of in the UK to sue one's own lawyer, so I never gave a thought to suing Urie Walsh and was anyway not aware of all the things he had done wrong professionally, pursuant to the California Rules of Professional Conduct. Why Urie Walsh did what he did, which Joel Belway should have spotted, will be incomprehensible to the vast majority of lawyers in California.

All this time I was not aware that Barbara was being fed information about the declining state of my business finances and indeed the mortgage situation in regards to the Bristol home. In retrospect I should have settled down to what would have become a war of attrition and rented a small flat in Napa with my own phone line, but I did not. I kept racking up hotel bills week after week while I was trying in my naivety to resolve the issue of getting meaningful access to my son. What I had not figured out was, whether in regard to Judge Grant or any of the other players, my right to see my son was the least of their worries: the only thing they had on their minds was that condominium.

The first supervised visit I had with Graham Jnr was for a few hours walking round the pond at the Marin County Civic Centre, with Barbara's sister-in-law holding his other hand. After that the court ordered the supervision be via a third party, so this became Mondays, Wednesdays and Fridays at a day care centre in Marin County, chosen by Barbara, from 1pm to 4pm, Barbara dragging Graham Jnr forty-five miles each way. She would sit in the proprietor's office watching us from a window in the building. This went on for weeks.

Now nearly six months after the abduction, Christmas was coming and the San Francisco Superior Court, Family Court Services and a private mediator recommended that there was no need for further visits to be supervised. Barbara brought him just once to where I was living in Napa—then unilaterally announced that the unsupervised visits would cease, and with Judge Grant in charge, implacably set against me, there was no way I could get any order enforced.

I had made friends with a rancher who lived up the Napa Valley and who had a small private plane based at an airport very near to the Salvador Child Care Centre. He offered to pick up Graham Jnr and me from the centre and fly us up to Canada where the British authorities had promised new passports for both of us. I thought about it for a while but concluded that the risks would not be worth the rewards. Even if the plan succeeded, the end result would be detrimental as my son would not be able to see his mother. I also could not see the American authorities letting us get away with such a plan. As I had already seen firsthand, abducting children is not the solution to the problem; whether I liked it or not I would have to work within the legal system.

When Christmas came, a visit was arranged at the only place Barbara would permit, that being her brother's home in Marin County, forty-five miles from Napa. I arrived on time with a present for my son. Upon my arrival Barbara's brother came out and insisted on my handing over my car keys. It was a cold day and Graham Jnr, being just over three and a half years old, kept complaining about it as we sat in the front of our rental car. I had thought we would be visiting his uncle's home, so of course he was not wrapped up for the cold weather and after a short period he asked if he could go indoors.

My visit had lasted less than an hour. When I subsequently asked him what he had done with the present I had brought him, the response I got was, "Uncle Don threw it in the trash."

Joel Belway and I went back to court. The best we could get was the court reinstating supervised access but with a change of place to Napa, and, to my surprise, an order that Barbara pay the cost of the supervision (she did not). However, this became another minefield where Barbara could play her mind games. She picked the Salvador Child Care Centre three miles out of Napa, and once she realised I was walking there, she would call the reception desk as soon as she knew I had begun my walk and give some excuse as to why my son would not be coming. This occurred once or twice a week.

One day Barbara and Graham Jnr turned up and I could see a heated exchange going on between Barbara and the owner of the childcare centre. When I went over I was shocked at what I saw. Graham Jnr's shorts were pulled down and all across the groin area and stomach appeared what looked like crocodile skin. It was a simply awful sight. The owner of the centre was insisting that Barbara take him to a doctor or the hospital, but Barbara was making out that she had no money to pay for such services. This of course was simply not true, but I stepped in and begged Barbara to take him to the local hospital. She agreed to do this if I called the hospital in her presence and offered to pay the charges, which I did. It transpired that he was suffering from a plethora of ailments, not the least of which was streptococcal pharyngitis, a potentially life-threatening illness.

The owner of the Salvador Child Care Centre subsequently filed a declaration with the court, outlining her concerns, not only with this awful incident but also Barbara's ongoing frustration of my access.

Concern for my son's welfare was forever in the back of my mind, this latest incident recalling others such as Barbara's refusal to pay for a car seat when we lived in England, and when we lived in the San Francisco condominium, coming back to find Graham Jnr toddling around our fourteenth-floor apartment with the sliding glass doors wide open. I had to get a carpenter in to block them off. At every instance Graham Jnr was held up to ransom for money.

Barbara missed several supervised access meetings at the

childcare centre with no explanation and in direct violation of my court-ordered rights of access. The owner of the establishment had also confronted Barbara about the outstanding fees that had accumulated, at which Barbara had stormed off having thrown the bill to the ground. Having no money because Coutts & Co. had refused to send any more to me, and because Joel Belway had ceased representing me, there was nothing I could do about it, so Barbara simply stopped bringing him to see me. It was pointless going back to court and citing her for contempt as there was no way that Judge Grant would enforce the order. There was no doubt in our minds that Judge Grant was using the supervised visitation issue as a way of punishing me for the appeals that Joel Belway had filed in regards to her orders regarding selling the condominium. This was an appallingly flagrant abuse of her judicial discretion—there is a presumption in law in California that each parent gets a 50/50 right of access to their children unless that is physically impossible, which was not applicable in my case—but there was nothing we could do.

There is another point where Joel Belway slipped up: as everyone was living in Napa County he could have applied to the court to transfer the file to Napa, which of course meant I would be out of the clutches of Judge Grant. I tried to get Family Court Services in Napa County to intercede but as they kept pointing out, they had no jurisdiction because the case was with the San Francisco Superior Court.

Then I made a mistake. After Christmas I phoned Barbara and asked why she would not let me see my son, to which she replied, "Give me the money and you can see him." She was goading me, and like a fool I drove to her home having had a drink, and kicked in her front door. For this I was subsequently given a two-day jail sentence, and although I am not excusing my actions, in my own defence the pressure on me at the time was simply more than I could take.

I had another big problem to contend with as well as this two-day sentence. Barbara and her lawyer had filed into the divorce proceedings an Order to Show Cause Re: Contempt. The 'Contempt' was my kicking down Barbara's door, which constituted a violation of the mutual restraining order. The Order to Show Cause was to be heard by Judge Grant at the San Francisco Superior Court. Not only was she my arch nemesis, but being taken to court again on this matter violated my double jeopardy rights as you cannot be convicted twice for the same crime, so as such it was unlawful. Unbelievably, that did not matter to Judge Grant and I was ordered to spend ten (the usual punishment for contempt is five days) in the San Francisco County Jail and to surrender myself by 1 April 1986.

I borrowed some money from a woman named Barbara Corotto, the director of Catholic Social Services, a local charity, to buy gas for my car and pay the toll charges for the Golden Gate Bridge, and travelled to the San Francisco City Hall, which was the same building that contained Judge Grant's courtroom. I knocked on the sheriff's door and spoke to him, explaining my situation. An outraged sheriff declared that there was no way I was going into his jail as I had already been tried and sentenced for the same offence in Napa County Municipal Court. He said that if Judge Grant wanted me there she would have to arrange it herself. So I knocked on Judge Grant's clerk's door and explained my situation to her clerk. I then heard Judge Grant's voice coming from somewhere in the back saying, "Tell him the contempt is purged." So I got into my rental car, travelled back to Napa and parked it at Fuller Park, where I spent the next three weeks sleeping in it.

It is perhaps worth bringing to the reader's attention that all this time I never had the benefit of today's easy communication by mobile phone, the Internet and e-mail. Transatlantic calls used to cost £1.00 per minute and a lot more from a hotel room.

As a way of alleviating the stress and boredom between going to court and trying to see my son, I attended Sunday services at a Baptist Church in Napa and became friendly with the Deputy Pastor.

# MY POSITION WAS SIMPLY HOPELESS

## Chapter 12

I was now well and truly on my own. My only hope was to get the San Francisco Superior Court to do as they had promised and agree to the return of my British passport. Unfortunately, even here the rules had changed. Judge Grant's clerk told me that the judge would agree to its return if Barbara's attorney agreed, but that was not the condition under which I had surrendered my passport, which was that I could have it back from the court at any time I requested it. However, I had no choice but to contact Barbara's attorney, Gail Connolly, and ask her to tell Judge Grant's clerk to let me have my passport. I was stunned at the reply: they would only agree to its return if I entered into a written agreement giving sole physical custody of my son to Barbara, and agree in writing never to return to the State of California, a condition I could not possibly accept as that meant I would never see Graham Jnr again.

Another spectre now raised its head at the same time as I found myself in this awful no-win situation. Barbara and Gail Connolly were now making claims on my British properties, the very same properties they had previously waived claim to in a letter written to Urie Walsh (who was still refusing to return copies of my files to me). I phoned Urie Walsh and literally begged him to call Gail Connolly and ask her to let me have my passport back. This he flatly refused to do. I asked him if he could at least send me a copy of the letter in which Barbara and her lawyer had waived all claim to my British homes so that I would have a home to go back to. Again he flatly refused.

I was in a Catch 22 situation; if I applied to the British Consulate for an emergency passport I would have been in violation of the court order wherein I undertook not to seek a replacement passport, and the British authorities could not give me one as they would need the permission of the San Francisco court. As I was now in Napa County, California, as were Barbara and Graham Jnr, I approached the court system there, but they could not help as they did not have jurisdiction. I was now well and truly stuck, and being *de facto* homeless, with no funds, I could do nothing to stop the condominium in San Francisco heading into foreclosure.

I had paid $256,000 for the condominium three years earlier and despite a rising property market it was sold on the auction block for $176,000. It was purchased by a member of the Ethics Committee of the State Bar of California, who subsequently sold it on for $473,000, making many hundreds of thousands of dollars in profit. It is now probably worth $1,250,000. The financial carnage was simply colossal.

It transpired that Barbara and Urie Walsh had turned up at the auction and it was reported back to me by Barbara that Walsh kept shouting, "Cook owes me money!"

As a result of Urie Walsh's failures and lies in regards to the first settlement agreement, the once excellent relationship I'd had with my bankers Coutts & Co. had deteriorated to the extent that all they wanted was the recovery of the funds they had advanced based on the first agreement. Of course, Urie Walsh's letter to them, falsely accusing them of impropriety when the lost envelope turned up in his office, was the final straw with the bank. Without notice Coutts & Co. refused to send me any more of my money or let me have any of what were my substantial liquid funds until I returned to the UK to sort things out. As a result of this, Joel Belway withdrew as I could not pay him.

At this point a light appeared on the horizon in the shape of my elder brother, David, who was in California on business, and it seemed likely he could come to my rescue. He offered to go and meet with Barbara to persuade her to instruct her lawyer to agree to the return of my British passport so I could go home. What my brother did not realise was that by telling her Coutts & Co. had cut off my funds and that I was working on a ranch cutting logs in return for room and board, she would quickly take in the fact that I was at my weakest. What he told her too was the name of the church I was attending, which was also attended by the parishioner who owned the ranch I was working on.

After he had met with Barbara, my brother met with me and told me that she had promised she would call her lawyer and instruct her to agree to the return of my passport. What in fact happened was that Barbara's brother phoned the deputy pastor of the church, Lee Wisdom, and told him the reason I could only see my son under supervision was because the court in San Francisco had ordered this on account I was beating him. Lee Wisdom then told this to all and sundry, including the owner of the ranch where I was working. I was given $100 and told to leave the ranch immediately. Only one of the local aid agencies, Catholic Social Services, would help me. Its director, Barbara Corotto, did not believe the story she had been told about beating my son. Nonetheless I was forced to go back to sleeping in my rental car at Fuller Park in downtown Napa. I phoned Barbara, pleading with her to let me have my passport back, and was told, "Nutso, don't call me again or I will phone the police".

I had found a true and helpful friend in Barbara Corotto—she continues to be an angel in my life to this day—who provided me with sustenance and coupons which allowed me to put gas in the rental car I still had—which was a worry in itself because, as I was not making the rental payments, I had the constant fear that the car rental company would report me to the applicable law enforcement agencies for auto theft.

I now no longer had a lawyer so I asked Barbara Corotto if she could recommend a local Napa lawyer who could help me get out of my predicament; she recommended Leonard Leushner who I had met on a couple of occasions. He promised he would represent me for free to get my passport back from the San Francisco Superior Court and see to the release of some of the money from the foreclosure of the San Francisco condominium. At last! Leonard Leushner was going to be my 'white knight' who would help me get out of this nightmare. It turned out that nothing could be further from the truth. His conduct proved to be just as despicable as some of my previous lawyers. Apart from all else, he turned out to be one of the most aggressive and verbally abusive people I have ever come across. The totally uncalled-for verbal abuse he hurled at me would spew out like a gushing tap or spigot. However, he was my only hope of getting out of California and back to England to regroup. I had no other options. I had phoned both Urie Walsh and Joel Belway pleading with them to help me, but to no avail: I was well and truly on my own.

It was at this point that I made another mistake. I should have surrendered to the Napa County Jail to serve the two days for kicking in Barbara's front door and at least got that out of the way. As it was, it came back to dog my steps later on. Had Leonard Leushner got me the money he had promised, from the sale proceeds of the condominium foreclosure, I could have rented a small flat and fought on in California without having to go back to England, and I could have served the two days in jail before the time set by the sentencing court was up. As it was, I was scared, hungry, tired, desperate and in a truly hopeless situation. Because of the expense I could not even afford a doctor or any medication to help me through this living nightmare. I had no choice but to agree to the terms and conditions as set out by Barbara and her lawyer so as to get my passport back.

The conditions were as follows, and are part of the court record and an order of the court. I had to put my UK home in Bristol up for sale and put the proceeds of the sale under the control of the San Francisco Court. I was told by Leushner that Gail Connolly had informed him the mortgage on my Bristol home was in arrears. I knew this but was taken aback by the extent of the information being fed to Barbara and her lawyer from Bristol. I asked Leonard Leushner to ask Barbara and Gail Connolly if they would contribute to paying off the arrears. The answer was no: to them the money from my Bristol home was a bonus. Barbara would also receive the remaining proceeds from the foreclosure of the San Francisco condominium and Urie Walsh and Gail Connolly would receive the outstanding fees they were alleging. What did I get in return? My British passport and $500 to pay for my one-way airline ticket; as it was put to me by Leonard Leushner, it was either that or go back to sleeping in the car.

I flatly refused to leave California unless I could see Graham

Jnr before I left as I had not seen him for three weeks. Barbara could not bring him to the Salvador Child Care Centre as she had refused to pay their bill despite being ordered to pay it, so she and Gail Connolly agreed I could see him, supervised by her brother and his wife at the Embassy Suites Hotel in Napa. I felt like a prisoner being guarded by two warders.

The conditions also stipulated that if I wanted to see my son in England for one month each year I would have to stay at my mother's cottage and pay for Barbara's round-trip airline ticket along with that of my son, and also pay her $5,000 towards her expenses.

What they were doing was crass stupidity on their part, because they were killing the goose that laid the golden egg by keeping me in no man's land in California while my businesses in the UK were failing, along with my credibility and financial standing. While they were concentrating all their efforts on trying to grab the money from the condominium and obstructing access to my son, I should have been at the height of my earnings power, but my earnings capability in the UK was rapidly going down the tubes. Barbara had the right, as was standard practice in California, to claim spousal support, which I would willingly have given, but all she succeeded in doing was stunting my earnings power.

So as to avoid any marriage liabilities in the UK caused by the abduction, and to distance themselves, Barbara and Gail Connolly insisted the marriage be dissolved with immediate effect that day, 22 April 1986.

With regard to my son I had three choices:

1. Try and forget him and get on with my life. But it was not in my character to quit, and anyway, what else was this debacle about if not being able to be a father to my son?

2. Stay in California and contend with Barbara's practice of holding my son out to ransom, consequently keeping me financially broke. Already I was sleeping in the car and had no money, so this was not a viable option.

3. Return to England and try to maintain contact by phone and mail, seeing him once a year in the UK. This held no attraction for the following reasons: my mental health, let alone my pocket, simply

would not be able to withstand the frustrations of Barbara's cruel 'phone hanging' technique; every year I would have the problem of paying child support, the cost of the phone calls trying to contact him, the cost of the two return airline tickets to bring him over, and Barbara's holiday expenses—this was assuming I could get employment to pay for these and was able to take a month off each year to be with my son; and every year, even if I had maintained contact by phone, Barbara would have had a whole year to destroy any chance of a decent father/son relationship. The annual visits to England would be a disaster, if Graham Jnr came at all.

In the end, unable to find a better alternative, I took the $500 and decided to leave California.

The passport was not handed back to me on the agreed day so I had to use some of the money for a hotel room and the transport to pick up my passport from Gail Connolly's office in Mill Valley. (This in itself was wrong as she should not have been in possession of it given the terms of its impoundment.) As a consequence I did not have enough money to pay for the airline ticket, so the British Government flew me home and confiscated my passport until I reimbursed them. Coutts & Co. had refused to send me any more of my money while I was in California, which is why I was unable to pay my new lawyer and my hotel bill. They wanted me back in Britain to sort things out there, and of course while stuck in California there was nothing I could do to force them to send my money.

I flew back into England on a Friday, and first thing on the following Monday my brother David's solicitor phoned the respective Coutts & Co. branch demanding the release of my money. I received a phone call that day from Coutts & Co. informing me it was available for immediate collection, but of course by then it was too late as the damage had been done. It was small consolation when I collected the money that a clerk followed me out of the bank to tell me how ashamed he was at the way I had been treated.

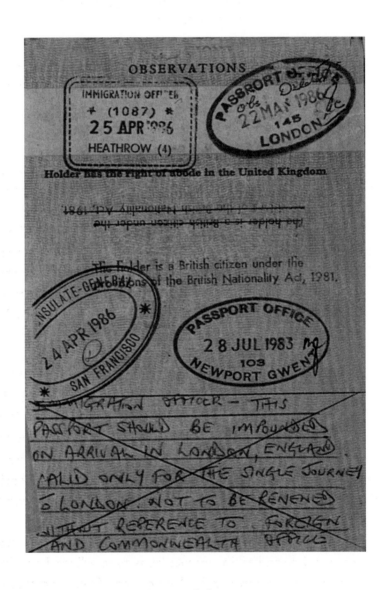

My impounded passport

# THE WARDSHIP PROCEEDINGS
# IN ENGLAND

## Chapter 13

Hindsight is a wonderful thing. Had I known what I know now, when I got back to England I would have regrouped, then gone back to California and not only challenged the unethical and illegal order forced upon me by Judge Isabella Horton Grant at the San Francisco Superior Court, but also sued Urie Walsh and his successor Joel Belway, for legal malpractice, as I successfully did years later. I make no secret of the fact that from getting on that plane back to England, I intended to do all in my power to get my son back on British soil and lawfully keep him there.

By this time I had gone along with the plan and complied with the San Francisco Superior Court order. I had put my Bristol home up for sale, put the proceeds from the sale within the control of the San Francisco Superior Court, arranged for the release of $5,000 to Barbara for her spending money, borrowed money from a new bank and pawned my Rolex to pay for the airline tickets for Barbara and our son. It transpired she had already contacted the San Francisco travel agent to discover if the airline tickets were cashable, but this was a loophole I had had the foresight to plug.

Inevitably, given the circumstances, I had to make plans that in the event that I prevailed in my wardship proceedings I would be living at an address unknown to Barbara or any of her cohorts in case she abducted our son once again, so I rented a house in Pulborough, West Sussex.

I engaged the services of a solicitor from one of the top London law firms, who in turn hired on my behalf one of the best family law QCs in the UK. I also needed a lawyer to testify to the events that had occurred in California—how I had been forced to succumb, under extreme duress, to the Californian custody order that had brought my son and Barbara to England. So I hired the services of a Californian lawyer, Robert Carrow, who had the distinction of also being an English barrister with chambers in London. I had met with him at his chambers and explained in detail what had gone on. This was to be the start of a legal, and also supportive, relationship that would last over thirteen years. I admired him for many reasons, not least because I saw myself in him. He was at one time the managing partner in his own law firm, one of San Francisco's largest. One day all the junior partners came to him en masse, demanding a better deal. He disliked what he saw as a bullying tactic and his solution was simple—he simply dissolved the law practice and became a solo practitioner again. Exactly what I would have done.

As regards Barbara, all we had to do was to get her and Graham Jnr on the plane to England. It was planned perfectly—with one exception: the London solicitors had forgotten to ask the most basic question, which was where my QC was going to be once we had served Barbara with the wardship papers. In other words, would he be available to make the necessary court appearances?

Barbara arrived at London Heathrow with our son in July 1986, and I was waiting with my mother. Overjoyed as I was to see my son again, I was even more elated to have Barbara on British soil as I knew that the wardship proceedings could then be initiated and I was confident I would succeed.

To my astonishment Barbara thought she would be staying at my mother's cottage. This was surprising for two reasons—one, my mother naturally did not want her in her cottage after what she had done, and second, as I no longer had my Bristol home I had no alternative but to stay there myself. My mother and I went back to her cottage with Graham Jnr and Barbara found herself accommodation in a convent.

After careful planning, Barbara was served with the wardship papers, but we had a big problem; the Queen's Counsel hired on my behalf by my London solicitors had gone off to France on a three-week holiday. Consequently I was required to instruct another barrister about what had occurred in California; this took place on a one-hour train journey on the way to court. Needless to say, without the stature of a QC representing me in this complex and difficult issue, and being offered instead a replacement barrister who knew nothing about the case except what I told him on the train journey, we lost.

We appealed, and lost that as well. Lord Justice Balcombe stated on the record that although he had great sympathy for the situation I found myself in when I had had to agree to the terms under which Graham Jnr came back to England, California was a civilised society with a well-defined legal system and his court could not be seen as a *de facto* Court of Appeal for the State of California. I would have to hand him back to Barbara and return to California to resolve the custody issue there. However, when overturning my wardship application, as a condition, Lord Justice Balcombe sought a specific undertaking from Barbara and her barrister that upon my son's return to California I would have meaningful access to him. They assented to this with no intention whatsoever of honouring it.

I was now saddled with all my own wasted legal costs and, as the losing party, I was ordered to pay Barbara's entire legal costs too.

On one of the most painful days in my life I returned my son to his mother and they flew back to California. As ordered by Judge Grant at our previous hearing in the San Francisco Superior Court, this all happened within the month.

The ticket for my Rolex watch, which I pawned to part-fund the wardship proceedings. I was unable to pawn it when I was sleeping in the car in Napa as it was being serviced in a jewellers in Bristol. I had thought I would only be gone a week.

# WHO NEEDS ENEMIES WITH A
# BROTHER LIKE MINE?

**Chapter 14**

**November 1986**

By this time, Barbara and my son had been back in Napa since the end of August, and Barbara had reverted to her usual tricks. Now flat broke and living in my mother's cottage, whenever I tried to phone my son she would either not answer, or answer it and leave it hanging. The latter was her preferred method because she knew that I wouldn't get to speak to Graham Jnr but I would end up with a huge phone bill. In this period I made hundreds of attempts but I didn't once get to speak to him. My businesses had ceased trading as a result of the time I had spent in California. My career was ruined. I was unemployed and broke.

On top of this I had three other problems looming. Firstly, Coutts & Co. were demanding that I sell my mother's cottage. Although I owed less on the mortgage than when I took it out (the mortgage payments were paid three months in advance and had never been late), Coutts & Co. wanted the cottage sold or they would foreclose on it to get their money back.

Secondly, the proceeds of my Bristol home were banked in the names of mine and Barbara's solicitors. I could not access them without doing two things. One was to go to California and try to prove to Judge Grant that Barbara had waived the claim to my Bristol home and the money was mine. This would be next to impossible as Urie Walsh was still refusing to return my files. Alternatively, I could go to the English courts and explain to a judge what had happened in

California and hopefully get my money back that way. However, if I had gone to the English courts again, whatever the outcome, when I subsequently returned to California to try and get access to my son I feared I would face more retribution from Judge Grant.

I would then have had three strikes against me. Strike one would be the debacle over the foreclosure of the condominium. Strike two would be my failed wardship proceedings in the English High Court. Strike three would have been my asking the English court to let me have the money from the sale of my Bristol home.

My concern was, whether I succeeded or failed to convince an English judge to let me have my money, I would have found myself in another Catch 22 situation. If I succeeded and got the money, Judge Grant would have punished me when I returned to California by either granting a contempt of court citation, or increasing my child support to some draconian level, or continuing to deny me proper access. All of this would have required me to hire English solicitors and barristers, or Californian lawyers, with money I did not have. If I failed, I would have been obliged to return to California to face that same Judge Grant. In every which way, I was boxed in.

My third problem was the two days in jail for kicking in Barbara's front door that I was due to serve in Napa County at the beginning of September. I had contacted Leonard Leushner and asked him to go and see the sentencing judge and explain my problem, that I had been obliged to leave California on 24 April 1986, and, even disregarding the money aspect, I still did not have a passport to get back into the US because I did not have the money to pay the UK government for repatriating me. It did not help that Leonard Leushner had turned out to be a Jekyll and Hyde. What he had told me in his car, going to court on 22 April, was diametrically different from his behaviour when we arrived at the courthouse. Here he had demanded to be paid $1,500 from the proceeds of the sale of the condominium that were being held in Gail Connolly's bank account. Without this, he told Judge Walker he would walk out. By this time I had used up the $1,500 Leonard Leushner had been given and now owed him a huge bill for all the work he had done in forcing Barbara to comply with the 22 April court order (and trying to get my golf clubs back). Leonard Leushner wouldn't go and see the Napa judge until I had paid off the new bill that had mounted up. I didn't have the money to do that. I had written to the court but had received no reply.

One Saturday morning I was at home when the phone rang. It was my brother David. Coutts & Co. were still bearing down on me to either sell my mother's cottage or get a new mortgage company. David told me he had an idea that would solve *all* my problems. If *he* bought the cottage from me this would get Coutts & Co. off my back, and with the remaining money I could go to California, hire a lawyer to get better access to my son and also prove that the money from the sale of my Bristol home was mine. I would have enough money to rent a home in Napa, get a car and make a fresh start.

What had originally started as a simple gesture by me, which would ensure that my mother and father lived rent-free for the rest of their lives, played no small part in my financial downfall. I purchased the cottage and also made all the mortgage payments and related expenses out of taxed income. Since my mother and father were classed as 'sitting tenants' under English law, the cottage was of no real value to me while they were alive. Whether they paid any rent or not, no one could evict them. In fact by law, they could pass that right on to one other living relative who occupied the property. As both my younger sister and brother qualified, in theory the cottage could have been tied up for over fifty years. So not only could I have not charged either of them rent, if they had decided to exercise their rights, I or my estate would be obliged to maintain the cottage at no cost whatsoever to them. I had acquired the cottage just a few weeks prior to my marriage to Barbara. If, as I have shown, it had no real value to me, that didn't prevent her wasting thousands of dollars of my money trying to establish a community property claim. Under Californian law, Barbara was theoretically entitled to half the increase in the value of the cottage.

After all the money I had expended on the cottage, I was now spending even more to defend my rights to it—a thing not only of no value to me, but in fact a liability. Nor could much be gained by transferring ownership to my mother. That would have led me into a quagmire of both English and Californian tax law. There was also the problem of Coutts & Co. and Urie Walsh. In the first case, Barbara and I had an unsecured overdraft which Coutts & Co. now wanted to see secured. In the second, Urie Walsh wanted to extricate himself and have his bill paid, come what may. That is why he cobbled together the first marriage settlement agreement and then lied about the outcome of the hearing designed to enforce it.

On their side, Coutts & Co., once they had secured our overdraft, and having realised there would be no money forthcoming from the condominium and with the stock certificates not appearing, saw only one way of retrieving their money and getting rid of me as a client. This was, to force me to sell my mother's cottage.

I didn't want to make a profit on the cottage as that would have undermined my reasons for buying it. The way I resolved this dilemma was to get my mother's blessing to sell the cottage to David. I agreed a knock-down price with him with the proviso that he would pay me extra money one year later if I needed it. All was agreed, and David said he would arrange for his best friend, a Manchester solicitor, to draw up the papers. It was also agreed that David would provide me with a cash advance so I could buy a ticket to California and try to see Graham Jnr.

David and I were very close, so my mother and I had every reason to trust him with regard to the purchase of the cottage. He had frequently stayed at my home and I had previously lent him the money—interest-free for a year—for the deposit on his first home, which he subsequently sold at an enormous profit. David was now riding the property boom with his own cottage in Greenwich, London.

I had already done a deal with the landlord of the rented house in Pulborough so that he could have all of my furniture in exchange for any rental termination penalties, and was staying at my mother's cottage to await David's solicitor preparing the papers. On a Sunday, David arrived with the sale papers which I signed and gave back to him. The plan was for him to personally take the papers to his friend, the Manchester solicitor, that day to speed up the sale so I could get the money more quickly. I decided not to have a solicitor represent me as I trusted my brother. I was ecstatic. I was going back to California to see my son. I would have money to hire a lawyer to get access to him, be able to rent an apartment in Napa, prove the money from the sale of my Bristol home was mine, *and* hire a legal malpractice lawyer to sue Urie Walsh. David gave me the advance for the air ticket and I caught the plane to San Francisco.

## 20 November 1986

It was late in the evening when I arrived in San Francisco and took the bus to Mill Valley where I checked into a motel. I chose Mill Valley because that was where Robert Carrow's offices were. As soon as I received the balance of the money from David I could pay Carrow a retainer, pay the outstanding fine in Napa, and do all the other things I needed to do. I immediately phoned Barbara and left a message on her answer phone telling her that I was back in California and asking if I could speak to my son on the phone. It was subsequently discovered that the next morning she contacted the Napa County District Attorney's Office to advise them I was back in California. A warrant for $10,000 was sworn for my arrest. This was for my not paying the $800 fine in Napa and doing the two days in jail.

I phoned Barbara again the next evening but when she answered she refused to let me speak to Graham Jnr unless I gave her my address. This made me suspicious and I refused to give it. She hung up. I tried again and found her answering machine switched on. From there on we were back to her not answering the phone. At this time I didn't know about the warrant, but I was still worried about the fine and outstanding jail time in Napa. I phoned the Napa County DA's Office, who refused to discuss the matter with me because I was not a lawyer. I then contacted Robert Carrow and he agreed to leave a message on Barbara's answering machine asking her or a lawyer to contact him. He also wrote a letter to Barbara making the same request, but he received no reply.

Weeks later I was still at the motel but had not received my money from David from the sale of my mother's cottage. He kept telling me that everything was going well with the sale and it was only a matter of time before he paid me. Meanwhile I had run out of money and had got myself a huge bill with the motel, which I could not pay until David sent the money he had promised. Even then I wasn't worried. I had still not been able to speak to my son and Barbara had not responded to any of Robert Carrow's messages. There was still in existence the court order of 22 April, which gave me telephone access to my son on Monday and Wednesday evenings. Barbara was not complying with that. This could not go on—Graham Jnr and I needed to talk and to see each other.

## 22 December 1986

In exasperation Robert Carrow sent Barbara a document entitled *Notice of Deposition and Request for Documents and Things* with a production date set for the shortest possible time. It was felt that this would flush Barbara, or a lawyer representing her, out into the open. I had been in California thirty-three days and had still not spoken to or seen my son.

## Christmas Eve, 1986

Although Barbara and what turned out to be her new lawyer—a Napa County man named Douglas Smith—knew of the existence of Robert Carrow as my lawyer, they made an *ex parte* application at the San Francisco Superior Court. This was for an order to transfer the money from the sale of my Bristol home from the bank account in England to an account at the Napa National Bank.

Robert Carrow was given no notice of the hearing or provided with any moving papers. Even more remarkable was the fact that the application and order violated every applicable rule of court and notice requirement. The subsequent order stated the following:

'. . . *it is further ordered that no officer, employee, or other person, with knowledge of this order shall notify petitioner or his solicitor, attorney, or any other person of this order until transfer of said monies above mentioned has been completed. Upon completion of the transfer of monies above mentioned, respondent's attorney shall immediately notify petitioner's attorney or solicitor of said transfer.*'

This type of *ex parte* order, i.e. an order obtained without either the other person or their lawyer being present, which a judge will sign simply because it is put under her/his nose, is endemic in California.

Douglas Smith used the Christmas period to fax the order over to Barbara's solicitor in Bristol—an order that violated every tenet of jurisprudence, decency and fair play. It subsequently transpired that not one single pejorative statement about me, used by Barbara and Douglas Smith to obtain the order, was true—and no bank account with the number designated existed at the Napa National Bank. The bank account number given to the court for the money to be wired from England was in fact Douglas Smith's own trust account.

My solicitor was informed and the order made in the San Francisco Superior Court was ignored. Had it not been, the bank would have left themselves wide open to a lawsuit from either my solicitor or me. The order was written in such a ridiculous manner that it even precluded the English bank manager or any of his staff from knowing about it, or anyone, for that matter, on Douglas Smith's staff, or even the clerk at the court, who had to endorse it. In fact the wording of it meant Douglas Smith violated his own order by faxing it to Bristol.

By now I had not seen Graham Jnr for four months. Barbara had her answering machine permanently on. Robert Carrow didn't know of the existence of Douglas Smith or of the order to transfer the money from the sale of my Bristol home, or the Napa County warrant. In desperation I decided to phone Barbara's brother's home in San Rafael. His wife answered and told me that my son was there. She asked for my phone number and promised my son would call me back. I asked why, if he was there, she couldn't put him on the phone there and then. I was suspicious and wouldn't give her my number. As it turned out, she was trying to get my number to give to the police to have me arrested and jailed over Christmas on the Napa County warrant for the unpaid fine.

## Christmas Day, 1986

I was completely out of funds. David had still not sent my money and I now had a huge hotel bill I couldn't pay. The fine too was still unpaid. I was behind on my child support and I could not see or speak to my son. I recall sitting on my motel bed drinking sugar water because I was so hungry—and crying.

After Christmas things began to improve a little. I was starting to get flak about my outstanding motel bill, but nothing aggressive. I had met a woman from Palo Alto who would come and pick me up and take me out. I was now employed doing some telemarketing. The pay was lousy but it put food in my stomach. Robert Carrow let me use his office phone to speak to David, who kept telling us it wouldn't be long before the sale went through and I would receive the cash. Robert's daughter and secretary, Amy, would let me borrow her car.

I was beginning to build a network of people whom I hoped would be the start of a circle of good friends. I had also found a contingency lawyer (no win no fee) who was prepared to sue Urie Walsh, and my solicitor in the UK had thwarted Barbara's attempt to transfer the proceeds of my Bristol home into Douglas Smith's bank account. I was making progress. All I needed was David to send my money.

## 9 January 1987

I had still not been able to talk to Graham Jnr on the phone and it was nearly five months since I had last seen him. Robert Carrow had now received a faxed copy of Douglas Smith's order and had phoned him. During the conversation he learned of the $10,000 warrant out on me in Napa County. Douglas Smith also told him that once the warrant was taken care of, there would be no problem arranging reasonable and ordinary access. It was agreed that Barbara would comply with Robert Carrow's request for the production of documents to be extended until 21 January. Barbara's proposed deposition would continue while we worked out an access plan. Robert Carrow and I thought that was it. Later that day he phoned the Napa County DA's Office to confirm there was a warrant and to make the arrangements to pay the outstanding $800 fine—and for me to surrender myself. But first I needed the money from my brother David to pay the fine.

## 21 January 1987

By now I had not seen my son for five months nor been able to speak to him on the phone. Later, I obtained the telephone records from the motel for the room I occupied for the period of 20 November 1986 to 21 January 1987. Using an independent witness I was able to show—by an analysis of the call duration—that on not one single occasion did Barbara pick up the phone, and that her telephone answering machine had remained permanently on.

At about 5pm I returned to my motel room. I had tried to arrange a business loan. I had got on well with the loan officer, who told me she would do all she could to help. My motel bill was still outstanding and the motel owner was agitated—but had not yet threatened to throw me out. In fact, I thought we all got on remarkably well considering the circumstances. The motel owner had spoken to David—everything I had told him was true—so he had no reason to doubt me. Two days earlier I had given him two personal cheques to cover my bill and asked him to hold them until David sent the money. He agreed to do this. It was explained to me that this would look better to the franchisers.

Then there was a knock on the door. When I answered it there were three detectives from the Mill Valley Police Department who explained that the cheques had been deposited and had bounced. The motel owner was also at the door. The officers asked to come into the room and for permission to search it. I had nothing to hide so I agreed. They suggested I get the friend from Palo Alto to run her credit card to cover the cheques. As I had only known her for three weeks and didn't anyway know her work phone number, that was out of the question. They then suggested I phone the loan officer at the bank and get her to bring the money to cover the cheques. It was late and the bank was closed so in no way would that solution have worked either.

I phoned Robert Carrow's office but no one answered. It was now 5pm—on a Friday night—and I didn't know anyone else who could cover those cheques. (I subsequently discovered that as I had been at the motel for more than thirty days I had obtained tenant rights. Theoretically, the motel would have to go to court to get an eviction order. Depositing the cheques had been done to put pressure on me and alleviate the need to go to court.)

The background check on me discovered the Napa County warrant. I now began to look like a criminal, even in the eyes of the motel owner. I was read my rights, arrested, handcuffed, transported to the jail cell at the Mill Valley police station and charged with defrauding an innkeeper. If I was convicted of this charge it could carry a sentence of up to five years in a state prison.

I was then transported to the Marin County Jail where I was searched, given orange coveralls, photographed, fingerprinted, given the proverbial phone call to my lawyer, and taken to my cell. There was a cruel irony to my being in this jail as it was in the same building, the Marin Civic Centre, where Barbara and I had been married.

# IN MARIN COUNTY JAIL

## Chapter 15

If you have never been in jail before it stands to reason you are likely to find it a disturbing experience. The first thing that hit me was I couldn't just walk out of the door. No matter what I did, I was not going to leave that jail until a judge or somebody else said I could. The second thing is that once that door slams behind you, there is no please or thank you, no privacy, no morality and no concept of right or wrong. However, I never once felt threatened by the inmates or guards, and I was never the subject of any cruel conduct. Marin is an affluent county and I'm sure things would have been different had I been in some other county jail. Yet this was still the last place I wanted to be—at any time, let alone in the middle of a custody dispute. This criminal charge subsequently set back my attempt at getting access to my son by years.

The cell I was placed in was built to house three people—but there were seven people in it, including me. The extra four had mattresses and slept on the floor. Three of my fellow cellmates were black drug dealers waiting to be transferred to Folsom Prison to start long prison terms. One was recovering from having been shot three times. In the cell there was a television, toilet and table. When you went to the toilet, anyone in the cell or anyone walking by could see you. The cell was spotlessly clean because that's the way the inmates wanted it. However, I was now entering a system with its own rules and conditions

One of the first things to happen when you enter the cell is that the other inmates want to know what you're in for. So I told them the whole story, finishing with my brother David, and they didn't believe me. None of them could believe that someone's own brother could do such a thing. The black guys thought I was in law enforcement put there to spy on them. I was saved when I had to go and see the probation officer. He was a nice guy and I asked him if a way could be found to get the judge to let me out. He told me he was sorry but there would still be no bail for me as I was considered a flight risk, and anyway had nowhere to go. And as he pointed out, I still had the Napa County warrant to worry about. I explained to him that I was concerned about my lady friend from Palo Alto—she might go to see me at the motel but wouldn't find me there. The officer took me to a phone so I could explain my predicament to her. She wanted to come and see me but I didn't want her to see me in this mess. Due to the length of time I was to subsequently spend in jail, this was the last time we spoke. I also explained to the officer the doubts that my fellow inmates had about my reasons for being in jail. He came back with a photocopy of my green card and told me to show it to them. You can't be in law enforcement and not be an American citizen, which obviously I was not. When I returned to the cell and showed them the photocopy it did the trick: they gave me no more bother.

Later that evening Robert Carrow came to see me. He explained what the charges were and what the procedure would be. On Monday morning I would be taken before the judge and bail would be requested—and be denied again. He would also speak to the District Attorney and the motel owner. My other concern was whether Barbara and Douglas Smith knew I was in jail, as obviously it would impact on my chances of seeing my son. The answer was yes— the Marin County Sheriff's Department had told the Napa County Sheriff's Department that they were holding me. In a small county such as Napa it was inevitable somebody would tell Douglas Smith. I asked Robert Carrow if he would put some money in my name at the commissary, the prison shop, so I could buy cigarettes, which he did.

After the meeting I was taken back to my cell. I started to become used to the routine—each morning a new disposable razor was handed through the bars by the sheriff's deputy and he would return a few minutes later to retrieve it. As the razors were so cheap and nasty and I had no shaving cream, I decided to grow a beard.

On the following Monday, dressed in my orange coveralls, I was taken from the cell up to the courtroom. I was not shackled like most of the other inmates. There was one—also on his way to the courthouse—who had been brought down from San Quentin State Prison on murder charges. I will never forget the sight of him—nothing but solid muscle covered in shackles.

I was so embarrassed as I entered the packed courtroom. My orange coveralls were about six inches too short and I was wearing sandals. I was placed on the front bench with all the other inmates and waited for the clerk to call my name. The practice was to call names in alphabetical order, so it wasn't long before I was in the dock before the judge with Robert Carrow by my side. He spoke discreetly in my ear, furious that I hadn't shaved and did not project an appropriate appearance (and of course, he was right). I entered a plea of not guilty and bail was denied. I was taken back to my cell.

Later that day Robert Carrow visited me in jail and told me about his meeting with Marin's District Attorney. The DA was prepared to dismiss the charges on two conditions—the motel bill had to be paid, and he wanted verifiable proof that I had been telling the truth about David (who had still not sent me my money). He also wanted to see a copy of the sale contract for the cottage and written confirmation from David and his solicitor accepting the blame for non-payment of the motel bill.

Little did I know that this simple demand would give David yet another opportunity to extract money from me. At this time I still had the services of a superb English solicitor, Norman Roberts, who was trying to fend off Coutts & Co. in their foreclosure proceedings on the cottage. This meant that because of David I was now accumulating legal fees with Norman Roberts as well as Robert Carrow, and if Coutts & Co. succeeded in the foreclosure proceeding, I would have to pay *their* fees and costs as well.

Robert Carrow's concern was that the longer this dragged on the more the chances were that the DA would withdraw his offer. The delays were beginning to make my story implausible. That would mean a full-blown criminal trial, and I would be in jail for months awaiting it. If convicted, I could go to prison. He also pointed out that the only way I could win the trial was to get David on the stand with the contract—but that was not going to happen. Also, as I was a resident alien of the US, a conviction for a felony would have subjected me to deportation proceedings and I would never see Graham Jnr again. There could be little doubt that Barbara and Douglas Smith would bring my conviction to the attention of the US immigration authorities. (It later became known that Douglas Smith had already contacted US Immigration, trying to get them to deport me.)

I began to settle into the jail system.

It was impossible not to notice that nearly every other word used by the black guys was punctuated by 'mother fucker'. Over a period of time this began to get on my nerves, so much so I conducted an experiment—one which indicated just what a motivator money is. I bet the worst offender $100 that he could not go twenty-four hours without saying 'mother fucker'. The deal was that anyone in the cell could call him any names, wake him up during the night, throw water on him etc. As he happened to be the one with the most violent past no one was going to be so stupid as to hit him. I then promised his two pals $50 if they could get him to use the forbidden words. As much as everyone tried he never once said them. What was also remarkable, considering his criminal past, was the sporting way in which he participated in the bet. Afterwards, there were no recriminations or bad feelings and I paid the bet when I later got out of jail.

Another thing that struck me was that nobody washed their hands after they had been to the toilet. Also, the black guys would sleep all day and then at about 10pm jump up and turn on the television to MTV—full blast—till 2am when it had to be turned off. During the day, if you were watching a television programme nobody, including the white guys, asked if they could change the channel: they simply got up and did it.

During the evenings the cell doors would open and new arrivals were escorted in. These were generally people who had been picked up on warrants. There were the usual inquiries as to what had led to the warrant and it was always someone else's fault. They would all claim to have good lawyers who would get them out within hours. However, I didn't see anyone get out within hours—most were there for days.

There were the little tricks you had to learn. For one thing, you did not take your pack of cigarettes along to the canteen because you couldn't deny you had any if asked by a fellow inmate. And by giving one away you couldn't refuse the others, so a pack would be gone at one sitting.

To return to David, who held the key to my situation in more ways than one—what was he up to?

After several weeks and dozens of phone calls between Norman Roberts, Robert Carrow and David's solicitor, Robert Carrow received a fax from my brother. His conditions were that he would only pay the motel bill and provide the written proof the DA wanted if I allowed him to take a consent judgment against me for the debt. A consent judgment is where he could sue me and I would not oppose his lawsuit. David's solicitor friend would attach a lien, or claim, against the bank account holding the money from the sale of the Bristol house. There were other strings attached and David added a whole litany of extra charges I had to pay. He wanted reimbursing for all his phone calls to Barbara, his solicitor's fees, the reimbursement for the airline ticket and just about everything but the kitchen sink—it added up to thousands of pounds.

What *exactly* was he up to?

He allowed Coutts & Co. to foreclose on the cottage and at the last possible moment bought it from them. He paid the combined value of the mortgage, the mortgage arrears to date, Coutts & Co.'s legal fees and the Robert Carrow liens (Carrow's legal right to use the property as security for a debt). He used the fact that it was his mother's cottage to get it at a bargain price. I never received a penny. David still owns it today. Because of my mother's financial circumstances she receives a cheque from the local council that covers the monthly rent, which in turn she pays to David. Of course when I owned the cottage my mother paid no rent, which was the point of my buying it. Meanwhile the value of the cottage has risen, pardon the pun, through the roof.

There was nothing I could do to stop the foreclosure, but I instructed Norman Roberts to attach a lien against the cottage in order to cover the legal bill I had run up with Robert Carrow. This he did. Unfortunately, Norman Roberts was legally precluded from attaching a lien to cover his own legal fees. I felt so sorry for him, a straightforward English solicitor who was unfortunately caught up in what had started out as a simple matter and had become a nightmare. He had been fending off Coutts & Co.'s foreclosure proceedings; was fending off Barbara's English solicitors who were trying to get the money from the sale of my Bristol home out of England; was dealing with David and his solicitor, and was also dealing with Robert Carrow who was trying to stop me from getting convicted on the fraud charge (this was 'defrauding an innkeeper', which carries a mandatory jail sentence). Meanwhile I was helpless, sitting in jail, laden with debts (I had the problem of paying the fine in Napa and was in arrears with child support along with a mountain of legal fees) and was still unable to see or speak to my son.

David and his solicitor had gone too far with their latest demands over the cottage and Norman Roberts threatened to ask the Law Society of England and Wales to intercede against them. Nonetheless, I had no option but to agree to David's terms and conditions, and I paid him all the money he demanded.

The motel bill was paid, the DA received the written proof he wanted and the charges were dismissed. After spending twenty-seven days in jail I was released. I was taken from the Marin County Jail, handcuffed, to the Napa County Jail where I remained until there was a court hearing and the warrant was discharged. Fortunately I was sentenced to time served. On a rainy Friday night Robert Carrow picked me up from the jail and put me up at the rundown Fireside Motel in Mill Valley. The first thing I did was borrow money from him to call Barbara and ask to speak to my son, to which Barbara answered, "What are you doing out of jail?" and refused. Douglas Smith had flatly informed Robert Carrow there would be no access to him until the money from the sale of my Bristol home was transferred to his bank account in Napa.

Regarding the not very white knight—my brother, David Cook,

who put me in jail and set my child custody dispute back many years—here I feel is a salutary lesson as to the perils that business done with family or friends can lead to. When I ask my mother whether he has qualms of conscience, she says he has none. He looks upon the cottage as his pension.

# OUT OF JAIL

## Chapter 16

Even though I was now out of jail, I hadn't a clue as to what I was going to do next. I had no money or possessions. I also did not have any court-ordered physical access to my son, or even phone access. I had not received a penny from the sale of Milton Cottage and Robert Carrow would not advance me any money, citing the grounds that it would be a violation of the State Bar Rules of Professional Conduct as it would be deemed to be supporting a client. He himself was to be paid from the liens he had placed against the title to Milton Cottage

Between one thing and another, my position was pretty bleak. I did not even have a phone in my room, so my days consisted of going to Robert Carrow's office to see if there was any progress, or hanging around in the reception area of the motel for that breakthrough phone call.

I desperately needed to find the money to get the divorce files transferred from the San Francisco Superior Court so as to get out of the clutches of Judge Grant, and hope that when the files got transferred to the Napa Superior Court I would get a fresh start with a new judge and the help of Napa County Family Court Services. It is difficult to explain the emotional state I was in as I not only had to find the money to keep a roof over my head, I wasn't seeing or speaking to my son and I had the task of trying to find a legal malpractice lawyer to sue Urie Walsh, who was responsible for this intolerable mess.

I managed to get a series of menial jobs on a part-time basis, selling hearing aids by cold calling from the telephone directory, working in an antique shop, a bakery, cold calling to arrange attendees at a child-rearing seminar and so on, while at the same time trawling my box of documents round from lawyer to lawyer in San Francisco trying to find someone who could grasp what Urie Walsh had done. One lawyer agreed to see me only while he was travelling on the underground from San Francisco to Oakland and even then I would have to pay his fare.

A problem I had was Urie Walsh's constant lying and illegal refusal to hand over my files. I found a lawyer, Albert Levy, who had agreed to take on my case and had filed a lawsuit on my behalf, but Walsh would only allow him to see certain documents in his own office where of course he tried out his well-worn lie that I had bounced a cheque on him. The result was that Albert Levy fell for this ploy and dismissed my lawsuit against Walsh.

I thought I had finally found an eminently suitable lawyer in Tom Low, as he had been the former Chief Prosecutor of the State Bar of California and had jointly written a book on Californian attorney ethics for a prominent and prestigious legal publisher. Tom Low had set himself up in private practice defending and suing lawyers in legal malpractice actions, or representing lawyers in the State Bar of California disciplinary proceedings. Week after week went by, which turned into months, where Tom Low continued to tell me he would file a lawsuit against Urie Walsh and litigate the case. But I had a time bomb ticking away. This was the statute of limitations on my action against Urie Walsh, as there would come a time when I could not sue him because my action would be time barred. By chance I picked up a newspaper and read that Tom Low had forged the signature of a Justice of the California Supreme Court on an order reinstating one of his clients to practise law; he had resigned with charges pending.

The big problem that would not go away was that every lawyer I had met had wanted to see the correspondence files that Urie Walsh was refusing to hand over. What I was doing was akin to asking a doctor to do a full medical examination while not being able to see the patient. What did not help was by that point I was a walking zombie, with Barbara and Douglas Smith forever up to their ruthless tricks and wearing me down. I did not have the benefit of medication for the anxiety, depression and severe lack of sleep, all of which I was suffering from. However, in the abyss I found myself in there were crumbs of humanity. A lawyer named Joe Hoffman, who could not help me professionally, asked at the end of our meeting if he could do anything for me personally as he could see I had something else on my mind. When I told him that my lifeline—my phone—was due to be cut off that night, without prompting he wrote out a personal cheque for $473 to cover the outstanding amount: a lot of money then, as it is today.

This unstable nomadic lifestyle went on for nearly a year while I clung to the hope that Urie Walsh would do the decent thing and settle my lawsuit against him. He did not. One day, while waiting at the bus stop to go into San Francisco to see yet another lawyer, I met a woman who became my girlfriend and who after a while asked me to move in with her and her sister in a little town outside of San Francisco known as San Anselmo. This relationship lasted about six months until she could not take the stress of all the litigation anymore. Then I had to revert to sleeping on the couch of a friend who was a ladies' hairdresser in Mill Valley, and also the couch of the pastor of a local church. To this day, the fear of not having a roof over my head still haunts me.

I must have seen over a dozen lawyers during this period, trying to get them to represent me, but Urie Walsh had either fobbed them off or they were unable to figure out just what he was doing. Finally, Robert Carrow, who was currently handling my custody issue, agreed to act for me in the legal malpractice lawsuit as well. At first he had been reluctant to get involved, but by now he was beginning to get a glimmer of understanding about what Urie Walsh had been up to, and agreed to take on my case. When, later, he instituted a new lawsuit against Walsh, we ran up against a statute of limitation problem caused by the dismissal of the first lawsuit filed by Albert Levy. Thanks to Robert Carrow's expertise the problem was overcome.

Unfortunately, Urie Walsh's refusal to hand over my files meant

Robert Carrow and I could not get the letter proving that Barbara and Gail Connolly had waived any claim on my Bristol home. Had we been able to prove this it would have meant I could have gone to court and obtained an order to transfer the remaining money. Then I would have had some funds to rent my own home. Alas, no letter, no money.

# THE LAW IN SMALL COUNTIES LIKE NAPA

## Chapter 17

Napa County is still small both in size and population. Although it may well be different now, most activity at the time of my involvement centred around the downtown area of the City of Napa. Lawyers' offices were found mainly around the courthouse and the jail, which consequently were out-and-out gossip shops.

After I had paid a fee, the files regarding the divorce proceedings were eventually transferred to the Napa County Superior Court. To try and force my hand, Douglas Smith and Barbara brought an Order to Show Cause Re: Contempt to get a judge in Napa to order me to agree to the transfer of the remaining money from the sale of my Bristol home into Douglas Smith's bank account. However, this failed, as Robert Carrow pointed out to me that my UK solicitor, Norman Roberts, had the power to ignore my instruction to allow the transfer if he thought my request had been made under duress. As Douglas Smith was asking that I be jailed for contempt if I did not agree to the transfer, Norman Roberts decided that without doubt my instruction was made under duress, so the order was unenforceable.

The problem with having to litigate in a small county such as Napa was the Californian law that required a judge to reside in the county in which they were elected or appointed. If you remember the television series *The Dukes of Hazard* you will know what the legal system was like in Napa. Being a small county, there was only a small pool of lawyers from which judges could be appointed or elected. There was also the issue of what motivated someone to want to become a judge. There were many benefits, not limited to the difference in income between what a practising lawyer earned and what they could make as a judge, which also brought with it an early retirement age and a lucrative pension, plus post-retirement income from secondment work for the California Judicial Council. Best of all was the availability of private judging for organisations such as the JAMS Foundation (Judicial Arbitration and Mediation Services, the USA's premier provider of private dispute resolution services).

I knew the Napa Superior Court had a terrible reputation with out of county lawyers for what was known as 'home-towning', defined in an American legal dictionary as:

*'Legalese for a lawyer or client suffering discrimination by a local judge who seems to favor local parties and/or attorneys over those from out of town.'*

The Napa Superior Court was also known for *ex parte* communications between the judges and a total lack of consideration to the needs of the litigants, especially those who were forced to represent themselves.

There was one hearing that sums up the cavalier attitude of the judges in this court. One of my lawyers, John Rothschild, and I were appearing before Judge Champlin and it became very apparent at the outset that the judge was not only not listening to John Rothschild but was reading the file that was next on the court calendar. It wasn't until John Rothschild respectfully pointed out to Judge Champlin that we had paid the court filing fee and the state was paying him to hear our case, that we finally got his attention.

Monday mornings when the courts were sitting was like a cattle market. The courtroom where all the cases were listed for hearing was always packed with what I guess to be about a hundred lawyers and their clients, with the lawyers sitting in what was the jury box. The names were called in alphabetical order and each side was asked how long they thought they needed for the hearing. Inevitably, Douglas Smith would ask for more time than he knew the court would have that week.

During this process the cases, where applicable, would be sent out to the respective judges, and the court would convene about an hour later, starting the process all over again with the remaining cases.

If there was no chance of a hearing, the persons without a hearing date that week were simply ordered to return the following week to go back into what was a lottery. It was a dehumanising process, especially for those people without a lawyer, who would not only be expected to address a packed room, but also tell out loud or listen to intimate details about their case being declared in public. You never even got the same judge for the same case. A simple appointment system would have alleviated this archaic method of operating and created a better chance of justice, but as a Napa County Court Commissioner once said to me, the Napa Superior Court operated like a fiefdom.

As a pointer to the low calibre of judges that small counties like Napa County produced, a short time later Judge Tisher, with whom I later had dealings in a unrelated matter, was publicly reproved by the California Commission on Judicial Performance for making a wilfully false statement on a critical issue in open court to one of the lawyers (as it happened, John Rothschild) who was before her. This was the same person who told me when she was still a lawyer that, "all new judges are bright and breezy for about three weeks after they are appointed, then they sink within the system." It did not take this judge long to sink into the moral morass that permeated the Napa County judicial system at the time.

There was another incident that illustrates this lack of integrity. One day I asked Judge Snowden in his courtroom, "Your honour, does it not worry you that people perjure themselves in your courtroom?" To which I got the following response, "No, Mr Cook, it happens all the time." I replied, "Your honour, it's not supposed to happen once." As to the moral turpitude of other local judges, the owner of the local rag, *The Napa Sentinel*, had files on all of them.

I cannot speak for what goes on these days because fortunately I am no longer caught up in their quagmire and there have been changes in the law, for example retired judges can no longer sit on the bench by assignment under the Assigned Judges Programme or operate as mediation judges for private organisations such as JAMS. However the problem still exists in small counties such as Napa County where inept lawyers can become judges.

# IN LIMBO

## Chapter 18

By now it was 1988 and I had two sets of litigation going on. One was my custody proceeding, which had been transferred to the Napa County Superior Court, and the other was my lawsuit against Urie Walsh for legal malpractice, which was at the San Francisco Superior Court. All this time I was not only broke or trying to maintain menial employment, I also had to find the money for the court fees, reporters' transcripts, travel costs, child support and at the same time sue Urie Walsh for walking me into this mess.

At this juncture there were three lawyers from three different law firms on my side, all of whom were involved in the custody proceedings. They would be paid provided I prevailed in my lawsuit against Urie Walsh: they were Robert Carrow, David Linden and John Rothschild. At the time, Rothschild was chairperson of the Family Law Committee of the State Bar of California. A fourth person, Peggy Schmeck, was intended, but we abandoned any plans for her to join the team when she came up with the proposal to file an 'Abandonment of Child' action, which meant I would have got out of this mess but lost any rights in regards to my son. She was another lawyer who on unrelated matters was eventually deemed ineligible to practise law.

The problem Robert Carrow and my other lawyers had was being able to get the Superior Court in Napa County to give us the time for a hearing, although because of 'home-towning', Douglas Smith and Barbara had absolutely no trouble finding court time when they wanted a court order to deny me access. Our problem in getting court time was due to there being a shortage of Superior Court judges. This was because California, in criminal matters, had instituted a 'three strikes and you're out' law, and mandatory sentencing. The result was that all the criminal elements in society were electing to go to trial, which resulted in a shortage because the Superior Court judges were the same judges who handled custody and divorce matters.

Another problem we had, which would permeate the whole of the time I was appearing in child custody matters at the Napa County Superior Court, was simply the laziness of the local judges, who put their needs before that of the litigants. As a result, files were passed repeatedly from judge to judge so that no one judge ever got a handle on what was going on. The file simply got thicker and thicker. I never ever saw any judge who asked to take time out to read the file or referred back to what was in it. So there we were, filing declaration after declaration with the court, pointing out, from the testimony of one witness after another, what Barbara and Douglas Smith were up to, but no judge had the time or the inclination to get to the bottom of things. Of course my own financial circumstances and not having a settled home meant I could not mount a change of custody application, so all my lawyers' time and my own time was devoted to trying to get a hearing and putting out the fires created by Barbara and Douglas Smith. I was a sitting duck.

# BARBARA'S MODUS OPERANDI

## Chapter 19

What follows is a short summary of what I had to contend with once I was back in California, which went on for nearly eight years. Keeping Barbara and Douglas Smith at bay was literally a day by day, week by week, month by month, year by year process, to which thirteen thick files at the Napa Superior Court and thousands of pages of documents testified.

## Judge Walker and my supervised access

After the failure of my wardship proceedings in the English courts, I had handed my son back within the allocated time. However, I had no court order to give me access upon my return to California. There was even a period during which the files were being transferred from the San Francisco Superior Court to the Napa Superior Court when I did not have a court I could go to. The result of this was that I had to agree to Barbara's terms for access, even as far as allowing Douglas Smith to interview the 'supervisors'. One supervisor was Barbara Corotto, who lived in Napa, and who was one of the most respected people in Napa County. Another was the pastor with whom I had become friendly, who also lived in Napa. The third was also a pastor, of a church in Lucas Valley, Marin County, forty-five miles from Napa, and the fourth was a local lawyer.

Having set up this complex web, Barbara and Douglas Smith would do their best to cause confusion by either misquoting what these people had stated or picking days and times when they knew these supervisors would be at work. This required another round of sworn declarations to be filed with the court, pointing out what

Barbara and her lawyer were doing, which, par for the course, no judge bothered to read.

There was one occasion when Barbara and Douglas Smith insisted that two supervisors were necessary, so Barbara Corotto had to pick up Graham Jnr and take him to Lee Shore, who was supervising me. They were so in control that we ended up in a situation where they were able to dictate the terms right down to the location. They once insisted I see my son at the offices of Barbara Corotto on a Saturday in the middle of the summer in a playroom in the loft of the office building where she worked. The temperature was measured at over 100 degrees Fahrenheit! Of course we did not use the playroom, but the choice of location illustrates the discomfort they were prepared to inflict. I suppose the hope was that I would give up or, equally important, that the people they had approved to do the supervised access would give up on helping me.

It was by now just before Christmas in late December 1987, approximately two and a half years after the initial abduction and one and a half years from when I had lost my wardship proceedings and handed my son back to Barbara. At this juncture Douglas Smith came up with a claim that there was a letter in existence written by me to Barbara after my return to California, in which I threatened to abduct our son. It was a ludicrous line of argument as, if that had been my intention, I would have done it while I had Graham Jnr with me in England and not handed him back at all. Douglas Smith refused to hand over the alleged letter, and it subsequently took Robert Carrow a great deal of correspondence to obtain a copy, which we finally received under the threat of a court order. This was the content:

*'Barbara, I spend seven days a week, twenty-four hours a day, all the money I've got, with one single intention, and that is to get my son back legally, that my son have a decent standard of living. He is not to be used as a pawn.'*

Yet again Douglas Smith turned out to be a liar.

The files finally arrived at the Napa County Superior Court and Robert Carrow filed an application asking that I be allowed non-supervised access. Monday after Monday when the courts were sitting we turned up, and each Monday we were turned away, being told there was no court time or an available judge. One Monday morning, however, when Robert Carrow and I arrived at the court, our luck was in and we were told that we had been allocated court time before Judge Walker. However, it was not long before our hopes were dashed as we were allocated only one hour. As this was my first hearing at the Napa Superior Court there was no way Robert Carrow or any lawyer could explain to the court in such a short space of time the convoluted history of events that had led us to this point.

Nevertheless, Robert Carrow put me on the witness stand and asked the simple straightforward question, had I ever written to Barbara threatening to abduct Graham Jnr, to which naturally I replied with an emphatic 'no'. Being on the witness stand allowed Douglas Smith to cross-examine me, and being aware that Judge Walker had determined at the outset how long the hearing would last, he went into time-wasting mode. The first question was, had I ever been a millionaire, to which I responded, what did Douglas Smith mean—a dollar millionaire or a British pound millionaire, or was I millionaire based on gross or net assets? This pointless line of questioning was brought to a halt by Judge Walker ordering Douglas Smith to move on as it had no relevance to my application to see my son, or Barbara's allegation about a letter from me threatening to abduct him. So off went Douglas Smith on another time-wasting spree, questioning me about the time I had spent in Marin County Jail. After a while Judge Walker put his foot down once more and ordered Douglas Smith to move on as that too had no relevance to my access request.

Inevitably, Douglas Smith's spurious questioning succeeded in its aim and valuable time was wasted. We did not have the time to call any of our visit supervisors, who could explain how they had been subjected to continual changes and interruptions. All we could do was rely on the subpoena Robert Carrow had served on Barbara and Douglas Smith to produce the letter in which they alleged that I had threatened abduction. Barbara took the witness stand holding the letter and Robert Carrow in cross-examination asked her to read out the relevant part. With glee she read out a sentence saying that when I had custody of our son we were going to live in Tiburon. As Tiburon is only about forty miles away from Napa and the letter also stated that I would be living there after I had custody, you could see Judge Walker look askance at Douglas Smith and ask, "Mr Smith, is this all you have got?"

Robert Carrow tried to move on, but our time was up and the best I could get was that Judge Walker ordered I have liberal access over the Christmas holiday, which was only days away. The case was adjourned for another hearing to be set down after Christmas. As Judge Walker would not be hearing family law matters the following year, this meant that we would have to start all over again with another judge. The file would subsequently be handed from judge to judge with the issues more and more obfuscated because the system was too cavalier to cater to the needs of the litigants.

So what did I get that Christmas? At Barbara and Douglas Smith's insistence I had two hours with Graham Jnr in the lobby of the Holiday Inn in Napa, supervised by a local lawyer who had offered to help me. I had also seen my son on two fleeting occasions in the study of George Scripture, a minister whose church owned the Montessori school which my son attended. When Barbara, whose friend was the head of the Montessori school, tried to stop this means of visiting Graham Jnr, George Scripture told the head teacher that if she attempted to do this he would terminate the school's lease.

## Barbara and Douglas Smith make a demand

Barbara and Douglas Smith made an offer that Robert Carrow and I could not refuse, as although I was living within a mile of my son's home and been back in California for nearly fifteen months, I had seen him on only eight supervised occasions for the sum total of twenty-seven and three-quarter hours and racked up a legal bill of $78,000. Barbara and Douglas Smith offered to drop the requirement for supervised access in return for the transfer of the money from the sale of my Bristol home to them, the bulk of the money being paid to Barbara. It did not dawn upon Judge Champlin that Douglas Smith and Barbara's demand for payment of money before I could see my son, in effect holding the child out for ransom, was in violation of the California Penal Code 207-2010, and in accepting the situation Judge

Champlin was acquiescing to this violation of the law. However, they had me over a barrel and we had no choice but to agree to their demand. What Judge Champlin could and should have done was to make an order that I could see my son and have telephone access without the necessity for payment. Still, for the first time, this court order at least gave me defined physical and telephone access to Graham Jnr. Within days Barbara was in violation of it.

## Barbara plays mind games using the phone access defined in the court order

Barbara was at it again. Although in return for my paying her the money from my Bristol home she had agreed to defined telephone and physical access, the court found her guilty of twelve out of twelve counts of contempt of court, and ordered the sentencing to be held over. But she was never sentenced. Neither did she ever pay a cent towards the legal fees that I was racking up yet again. So, on the next set of contempt of court proceedings, the court accepted our proposal that Barbara Corotto sit in Barbara's home at the designated times to make sure the phone was picked up and I could speak to my son. This worked for a while, but it could not go on forever, so as this system began to fail, Barbara went back to her usual modus operandi. In fact, on the court record there are over one hundred and fifty-six separate specified times in various applications for Order to Show Cause Re: Contempt where she had violated my defined rights of access. But she was never once ordered to pay a dime in lawyers' fees or suffered any punishment, as the courts would not find the time.

## Within weeks Barbara and her lawyer vary the order

Without notice, within weeks after the money from my Bristol home had come through and the new unsupervised access order had been entered, Barbara and Douglas Smith were able to obtain a restraining order banning me from going within eight hundred yards of her place of work or Graham Jnr's school—which naturally prevented me from picking him up from either place—and banning my phone access. Yet again I had to rack up lawyers' fees to get the order reversed. Every time they wanted to get a court order to stop my access, Barbara and Douglas Smith always got a court hearing, but the same rule never applied to us because of home-towning. You may also ask how it was possible for Barbara and Douglas Smith to get a restraining order denying me the selfsame phone and physical access that the court itself had agreed to only weeks earlier after I had paid the ransom: the sale money from my Bristol home. The simple explanation is that it was a different judge from the one who had granted the original order and judges will sign restraining orders at a drop of a hat just to protect themselves in case something were to happen. Over and over again we were back to square one.

## Barbara stated she had a recording on a telephone answering machine which proved my son did not want to see or speak to me

Barbara claimed she had a tape—which took Robert Carrow months to force her to finally produce with the threat of a court order—on which my five-year-old son could be clearly heard saying, "I hate you, I hate you, and I never want to see you again. Don't phone me." I took the tape to the Robert Plant recording studios in Sausalito and asked if they could enhance it. Sure enough, word for word, Barbara could be heard in the background telling my son exactly what to say. Did the court at a subsequent hearing take any notice of this tape and what Barbara had done? No, it did not.

## Barbara and Douglas Smith continue to be obstructive

I had made an application to the court to have Graham Jnr during the forthcoming school summer break to go to Lake Tahoe in northern California. This was inevitably opposed by Barbara and Douglas Smith, even though the alternative was for him to be looked after by his very elderly grandmother in her one-bedroom flat in Napa, which did not even have air conditioning, and they put forward all the usual mantra as to why I was not capable of looking after him. Mind you, in Barbara's opinion I had been perfectly capable of looking after him years earlier when she had brought him to England and I had paid for the round-trip air tickets for her and our son, and given her $5,000 in spending money! There was no evidence before the court or elsewhere that I was not capable of looking after him.

When Judge Champlin set the matter down for a hearing the following Monday, Douglas Smith objected, stating he would not be available as he was going camping with his children. At this, Judge Champlin exploded and told Douglas Smith that time was of the essence and all he could see was a father trying to have a holiday with his child. He told Douglas Smith that either he would have to be there the following Monday or arrange a stand-in. Then he adjourned the hearing for half an hour and ordered us all to go out into the corridor of the courthouse and sort something out. There we had a situation where Douglas Smith and John Rothschild were eyeballing each other and metaphorically going toe to toe. As things grew heated, up popped a huge Napa County Deputy Sheriff to stop things turning violent, and from that time on, when Cook v. Cook was on the calendar, this Deputy Sheriff was always on hand in the corridor.

Douglas Smith said he could not arrange a stand-in so he capitulated and I was granted my summer access. As I was to find out later, he and Barbara made sure there was a payback for this humiliating about-turn.

It always intrigued us as to what was motivating Douglas Smith in his obsession at stopping me having access to my son, which as time went on became even more extreme. In fact one of his partners, Rebecca Yost, was overheard at a Napa County Bar function saying she could not understand Douglas Smith's obsession with the case. We can only speculate as to what was going on between Barbara and Douglas Smith, but the one thing we can ascertain from this incident is, they could either not find a lawyer willing to stand in on this meaningless attempt at obstruction, or they would not lay out money on another lawyer.

## I go back to England to regroup

The necessity to go to England was because my sister Alison, staying at my mother's home, was dying of cancer. Before leaving the

USA I had requested, through my lawyer John Rothschild, that the times of my telephone access in the court order be changed to accommodate the fact that the time zone in England was eight hours ahead of California time. Barbara and Douglas Smith flatly refused to do this. So for the eight months that I was in England I had to stay up until 3am every Monday and Wednesday hoping and praying that my son would be there to answer the phone. Sadly, most of my attempts at speaking to him were fruitless.

It was also very unfair on my sister, who would sometimes be disturbed by hearing my voice at three in the morning. This was because I was staying at my mother's small cottage and making the phone calls from the living room on the ground floor, while she was upstairs, very ill. I still have the vivid memory of my mother banging on her bedroom floor asking me to keep my voice down on the few occasions that I managed to get my son on the phone. I had returned to California when she died.

While I was stuck in England I was racking up unpaid rent with my landlady in Tiburon, California. Other matters also made my return inevitable. The first was that my ex-wife Jane, who still lived near Bristol, brought our twin daughters to visit me—the one and only time—at my mother's cottage in Charlbury, to ask my permission to take them to live in the Canary Islands. Although I would no longer be able to physically see them, we had joint custody and she faithfully promised liberal access rights, so I agreed.

The second difficulty was that the UK tax authorities, the Inland Revenue, had made me bankrupt on account of all the tax I owed, so I would not be able to start a new business in the UK for three years, or even have a bank account, and the bankruptcy would remain on my credit record for years. But I could not remain in limbo at my mother's cottage racking up a phone bill for calls to the USA at £1.00 per minute.

Then I had the problem of Urie Walsh: I had to go back to take care of the litigation against him. In this there was a double thrust to Urie Walsh's stunning intransigence. He had what was known as a declining balance legal malpractice insurance policy, so while he was fighting Robert Carrow and me into the ground, the cost of his defence was coming off the amount of his insurance cover, which meant that there was less and less to be paid to me. All in all I had no choice but to return to California, even though the very thought of it terrified me.

## I return to California

I had managed to sell the rights to my story to the *London Daily Telegraph* magazine, which meant that I could fund my return and, importantly, pay my child support arrears and the outstanding rent to my landlady in Tiburon. The very first thing I did on the Friday I arrived back in Napa, after checking into my hotel room, was to contact my caseworker at the Child Support Division of the Napa County District Attorney's office to inform him I was back and where I was staying, and assure him I would be down first thing Monday morning to pay my child support arrears. I then called Barbara and left a message saying that pursuant to my court-ordered access I would be picking up my son the next day. Because I suspected there might be problems enforcing my rights under my court order, I contacted the City of Napa Police Department and requested a police officer to be in the background.

When I arrived the next day, the first words Barbara spoke to the police officer were, "What's he doing here when there is a warrant out for him?" When the officer checked, sure enough there was a warrant for my arrest, sworn the day before, charging me with 'child neglect'. Of course it was totally illogical as to how I could be charged with child neglect when at the time I was 7,000 miles away and the instigator of the criminal complaint, Barbara, had the child in her care at this time. But logic did not come into dealing with what was going on in the Napa court system in those days.

Unbelievably, I was handcuffed and taken to the county jail where I stayed for a few hours until my friend Barbara Corotto could get hold of my lawyer John Rothschild. He managed to contact the Napa County weekend duty judge, the Honourable Ron Young, who phoned the county jail and ordered my release by dropping the bail. Barbara and Douglas Smith's plan was that I would remain in the Napa County Jail until any forthcoming trial.

When I returned to Barbara's home late that morning with a police officer in attendance, neither Barbara nor my son was there. But in an egregious encounter outside the courtroom at the first hearing, the Assistant DA, a friend of Douglas Smith, told me he would 'get me whatever it took'.

On the Monday I travelled to Tiburon with the intention of paying my rent arrears and hopefully resume occupation of my little flat. The landlady, however, was no longer friendly towards me although we had been on totally amicable terms when I left for England. When I offered to pay the rent she refused to take the money or discuss the matter. I was puzzled.

The 'child neglect' charges were simply bogus and subsequently dismissed. However, this emphasises how endemically corrupt the Napa County legal system was. Even the caseworker at the child support division who had the warrant for my arrest sworn against me was later forced to resign for requesting sex and drugs from clients for preferential treatment in collecting child support. On top of that, the same Assistant District Attorney who had prosecuted me got caught up in a scandal because he tried to buy alcohol out of hours by flashing his Assistant DA badge.

## Things did not end there

Upon my return from Tiburon I was faced with another application to the court to withdraw my access rights. This was supported by declarations, prepared by Douglas Smith, from the wife of a neighbour where I was staying at Lake Tahoe, claiming I had stolen her motor vehicle. In reality, I had borrowed it with her blessing. As she had spent vast amounts of her life in and out of mental institutions and didn't turn up for the hearing, the court ruled that Douglas Smith's prepared declaration was worthless.

The next attack came from a different angle: the owner of the property I had rented in Lake Tahoe declared I had fed my son only chocolate bars and hamburgers. In fact she had spent very little time with us and, when we did meet with her, it was in a cafeteria-style setting as we were on vacation. She too failed to turn up for the hearing and Douglas Smith's prepared declaration again proved worthless. This left me with Douglas Smith's third prepared declaration which concerned my former landlady in Tiburon to whom I had tried to pay my rent arrears. Douglas Smith had lined her up to testify against me and my attempt at paying my rent arrears was turned around to an attempt to pay her off as a witness; this transparent lie, too, was seen through. But this lady had her own demons to deal with: she had spent seven years helping her boyfriend day and night to obtain custody or reasonable access to his children. As soon as the objective was achieved, what did he do but go back to his ex-wife, leaving her high and dry, seven years of her life wasted.

Additionally, we had recourse to a third party who testified that she had told Douglas Smith that in her opinion I was an excellent father. All these attempts to stop me seeing my son consequently failed dismally.

## Clutching at any straw to obstruct access

Barbara finally tripped herself up by telling one lie too many. One particular Sunday I spent the day with Graham Jnr next to a swimming pool. It was a magnificent sunny day and next to us was a very attractive woman who, as I soon found out, had just ended a four-year relationship. As much as I tried I could not get a date with her. At the end of the day, when we all parted company, the only thing I had found out was where she worked. The next morning I got a phone call from one of my lawyers, John Rothschild, who told me that Barbara and her lawyer were going to get a court order denying me access because, apparently, when I returned him to his mother he was so sunburned he could not go to school. Realising I had the means of disproving their story, I contacted the woman I had met the previous day and, knowing what she did for a living, asked if she would testify on my behalf. At the hearing Barbara and her lawyer put forward their case. John Rothschild called my recent acquaintance to the witness stand. Her testimony was that she had perceived me to be, if anything, overprotective of my son, not negligent, and that the boy was not sunburned in the slightest. A mighty testimony indeed from a witness who turned out to be the Child Protection Officer for Napa County!

# KATIE

## Chapter 20

For quite a long time, about four years, I was fortunate to be living with a woman named Katie. It came about when, one day in early 1989, I was at the bar of the Holiday Inn in Napa and a very attractive woman approached me and challenged me to a game of 'Liars Dice'. The rest, as they say, is history: we ended up living together at her home in Sacramento.

Katie was much younger than me, divorced with three children, beautiful, a dedicated and superb mother, incredibly intelligent, well-educated, well-paid, exceedingly good at her job as a fraud investigator for the Department of Education for the State of California, and most of all totally committed to me and my objectives. My living with Katie was Barbara and Douglas Smith's worst nightmare. I not only had the emotional benefit of being with Katie but I also had a roof over my head, plus the advantage of Katie's excellent typing skills, which were essential for all the documents that had to be prepared and filed with the court regarding my custody dispute. Just as crucial was her help with the all-important third-party mailing of legal documents to Douglas Smith.

Never one to take more than I could give, there was a practical trade-off in my relationship with Katie in that she travelled a lot on business, and while she was away I would occupy the time, when not in court, doing up what had been the most derelict house on Katie's housing estate and turning it into the best house in the area. I would also look after her three children aged fifteen, thirteen and nine, along with Graham Jnr, who was ten.

In 1992 Katie was away on business for virtually the entire

scorching hot summer, so from first thing Monday morning to late on Friday I looked after all the children. We had a routine: after breakfast the children would do their tasks around the house, then I would provide supplementary homework to keep them up to scratch for when they returned to school. Not being a trained teacher I had to devise my own curriculum and we concentrated on two main areas. Each child chose a section from the *San Francisco Chronicle* and then picked an article to explain to the others what they thought were the implications of the article. The other was to get them to write letters to Amnesty International about detainees we had read or heard about. This meant not only were we doing a good deed but I could also correct their grammar and spelling. Katie's children liked the routine and in particular that they always knew where they stood with me.

When this part of the day was over off they would go off to play, either with each other or the kids in the neighbourhood. Then we would get to the part of the day they liked most all. Four 'rug rats' would lie in front of the television with a huge bowl of ice cream with all the toppings, and we would watch the old television programmes such as *Bonanza*, *The Rifleman* and *The Big Valley*. Then the fun would start. When the children asked for second helpings I had a fictitious 'nasty' twin brother who might or might not appear from the kitchen. If it were me it would be with extra portions of ice cream. If it were my 'nasty' twin brother he would appear with his high-pressure, high-volume power ware pistol which the children also had on hand. Then war would be declared with all of us hunting each other down, often for hours and sometimes vast distances from home—many betrayals—no holds barred. If Katie returned during the week she would join in the game. Sometimes the children and I would hunt her and give her the 'Chinese punishment' where she would be staked out and given the water treatment. Just as likely the tables would be turned and I was the hunted one with Katie the instigator.

At one time Katie and I decided it would be great if we had some pets for our children as we had a large backyard. We got some rabbits, chickens, Billy the goat, and best of all a skinny, flea-bitten female puppy which we called Smokey. Smokey was beautiful, intelligent, outgoing and loyal, and was soon perfectly trained. She was the dog most people would dream of having as a pet. She loved the children and they loved her and we all went everywhere together. However, Katie did not believe dogs should sleep in the home, so Smokey had to sleep in her basket in the garage. This was not a problem for her because when Katie was away she slept in the children's bedroom and Katie was none the wiser. When she was home a different routine was played out. Before going to bed I would wait until I could hear Katie take a shower then open the door from the garage to the living room. Smokey would scurry across the living room and dart under one of the children's beds. In the mornings it was the same routine but in reverse. The children would hear Katie taking a shower and let Smokey out so she could scurry back to her basket in the garage.

When I used to take Smokey for a walk, I would affectionately speak a unique phrase to her, using my English humour. One day I asked Graham Jnr to take Smokey for a walk and heard him repeat my exact same words. A parent is so much a role model for a child!

Katie's support of me was unremitting: she would take time off work to attend all the court hearings and spent virtually every evening and weekend helping me with typing and photocopying. As we got deeper and deeper into what can only be described as Barbara and Douglas Smith's pathological desire to thwart my access, in two years we put over 80,000 miles on Katie's car going up and down the freeway to court hearings and meetings with family court services, lawyers and counsellors. Our problems were exacerbated by the distances between the respective courts and where we were living. The Napa County Superior Court is approximately 80 miles from Sacramento, and the San Francisco Superior Court, where I was suing Urie Walsh, is approximately 125 miles from Sacramento. It was literally a full-time job, and to fund my legal endeavours Katie took out one mortgage after another against her home.

## Barbara and Douglas Smith attack relentlessly

We continued to be harassed by Barbara and Douglas Smith, who had yet another trick up their sleeve to try and get me, once and for all. To explain their next move it is best to explain the law. To bring an 'Order to Show Cause Re: Contempt' the moving party has to specify what order has been breached, then specify the alleged breach and when it happened. This is critically important as the defendant is at risk of going to jail and is required to defend himself against each alleged breach of the specified order. What was interesting was that, as far as my lawyer and I could deduce, my alleged infractions were all related to my attempts at seeing my son or asking Barbara if she would see reason.

It fell out that the Order Re: Contempt hearing was to come before the Honourable Richard A. Bennett. This judge had made no secret of his dislike of me and had a reputation of being a swaggerer who would not read anyone's file, let alone mine. The result of the hearing was that, incredibly, I was found guilty of all the alleged contempt charges. I was sentenced to 90 days in the county jail and ordered to pay Douglas Smith $18,000 in attorney fees.

This sentence disregarded the legal requirement of my right to file an income and expense form so that the court could adjudicate whether or not I could pay, and Douglas Smith did not produce any billing records to support the $18,000 he had been awarded. The applicable higher authorities appointed a lawyer to represent me free of charge on appeal and in the end I did not serve one day in jail for this, nor did I pay Douglas Smith one cent of his money. However I had to put up with the stress and anxiety of this situation for well over a year.

Barbara, who had actually been found guilty of a plethora of contempt citations, paid no fines, attorney fees or jail time; she had got away scot free because of the 'home-towning' that went on in this Dukes of Hazard-style county.

## The bin man

With or without a court order, one thing was for certain: Barbara and her lawyer would do all they could to ruin any time I had with my son. They used the services of a part-time fireman, a friend of Douglas Smith, who used to act as a process server (a person empowered to serve legal papers). When I would arrive at Barbara's home to collect Graham Jnr, time and time again this part-time process server would jump out from behind the garbage bin and serve me with whatever legal manoeuvre they had dreamt up. The normal practice would have been to serve my Attorney of Record, John Rothschild, with the papers, not jump out at me from hiding places. We ended up stopping this ridiculousness by getting a court order. It is an irony that sometime later I happened to be at the Napa Superior Court where I witnessed this process server being sentenced to state prison for molesting his stepdaughters.

## They play tricks all the time

If I turned up early at Barbara's home she would wait until the exact time stated in the court order to produce Graham Jnr. If I turned up late due to traffic or for some other reason, they would be gone. Then there were the times when I would turn up to be told untruthfully that he was ill. On one occasion a Monday phone call with my son revealed that, while he was supposed to have been ill on the previous weekend, he and his mother had been to Disneyland. There was also a refusal to provide copies of his school reports or even to say who his doctor was. But if I was late with the child support, she was onto that like a shot. The trouble was I could not get a court hearing, and she knew that if she was found guilty of contempt of court, nothing would be done.

## Picking up Graham Jnr

As part of her duties Katie would often travel south of Napa on business and for a while would pick up Graham Jnr from Barbara's home on a Friday night and then head home to Sacramento, 80 miles away. We had only the one car, so Barbara and Douglas Smith got a court order stating that I was the only person allowed to pick him up, which meant as soon as Katie arrived home on a Friday night I would have to head south to Napa driving all those miles each way. Their plan was even a bit more Machiavellian than that: Katie had to plan her business day to make sure she got back to Sacramento in sufficient time for me to get to Napa, because if I did not arrive in Napa for the court-specified time, Barbara and Graham Jnr would be gone.

## Freddy Krueger

Barbara and Douglas Smith came up with yet another set of reasons to try and deny me access. They claimed that when I had Graham Jnr at weekends I was allowing my nine-year-old son to stay up late watching X-rated Freddy Krueger films; also that he was slipping out at night to go to a nearby river creek. Apart from the fact I have never seen a Freddy Krueger film in my life and the river creek was a total figment of their distorted imaginations, after we went through this legal hurdle it turned out my son was watching the Freddy Krueger films and going to the river creek at his mother's home.

## Katie faces a criminal charge

Barbara and Douglas Smith could not stand Katie being in my

life because of all the support she gave me. However, she had something of an Achilles heel, as, being a Certified Public Accountant and fraud investigator for the Department of Education for the State of California, any criminal conviction would put her licence and career at risk, and here was I, forever involved with people who would go to any lengths to achieve just that. The significant factor here is that she was working for me as an *in propria persona* litigant, i.e. I was representing myself and as such was afforded under the law all the rights of a lawyer in the litigation process. Katie never personally served any legal documents. This is a critical factor with regard to what was to happen next.

One day we received a phone call from the City of Napa Police Department advising us that Katie had been charged with violating the law, insomuch as she had served over ten legal documents in a one-year period without being a registered process server. This law was so obscure that since its enactment in California not a single case appeared on the record to show anyone had been prosecuted under it. Apart from that, the purpose of the law was to cover people who were paid a fee to serve legal papers, so it only related to personal service, not to servicing my mail as she had been doing. Lawyers, secretaries, etc. were exempt, and thus Katie was exempt too, because I was representing myself. When contacted, the people who had proposed the original bill before the California legislature were furious at this abuse of what their law was intended to prevent and volunteered to testify on Katie's behalf at any forthcoming trial.

It was election year for the Napa County District Attorney. The story about Katie's prosecution and the waste of taxpayers' money that this represented hit the front page of the local tabloid newspaper on a Friday. The following Monday, in court, just as Katie's arraignment was taking place, the courtroom doors burst open and in stormed a man, small in stature, big with fury, who grabbed the file from the Assistant District Attorney and said to the judge, "Your Honour, my name is Jerome K. Mauntner, District Attorney for Napa County, California. I read about this case in the newspaper and upon investigation have concluded that the defendant has committed no crime and should never have been charged. I am dismissing the case."

Whereupon he threw the file back into the hands of the Assistant DA and stormed out.

In the end, all the typing, research, filing with the court and all our legal endeavours turned out to be a complete waste of time and expense as no judge could be bothered to read the whole file. When we prepared an extensive document which took over six months to produce, it was met with derision by the judge who was asked to take it into account.

### Barbara and Douglas Smith still keep trying to split us up

What Barbara and Douglas Smith wanted to do was to drive a wedge between Katie and me so I would lose her incalculable support. They therefore came up with another ploy, a subpoena to force her to appear in court to testify about my finances on yet another Order to Show Cause Re: Contempt—technically I owed Douglas Smith the $18,000 which was still on appeal. Although it was not a matter that would be heard by the Napa Superior Court, Douglas Smith wanted to try and prove that she was supporting me, and that she might be able to prevent me from going to jail by stumping up the money. He served her with a subpoena which compelled her attendance in court. The problem was twofold: every time, as required by law, she requested her witness fees, Douglas Smith refused to pay them. At the same time, under the guise of the selfsame subpoena, he demanded—under threat of imprisonment, no less—that she keep coming back to court week after week as the case was waiting to be set down for a hearing. All this, of course, required her to take time off work to appear on the Monday mornings when the matter was being called on the court calendar.

After many weeks Katie turned up in court yet again. What I saw that day was without doubt the best lawyering I had ever witnessed. I was being represented by the Napa County public defender as Douglas Smith had brought an Order to Show Cause Re: Contempt for my failure to pay him all or any of the $18,000 in attorney fees I had been ordered to pay by my arch nemesis Judge Bennett. What Douglas Smith wanted was to get Katie on the witness stand where she would have had to testify that, given a choice between me going to jail for contempt, or paying the fees on my behalf, she would have stumped up the money. Robert Carrow had agreed to represent Katie on the issue of Douglas Smith refusing to pay her witness fees. Being aware that a judge only has jurisdiction in the courtroom, Robert Carrow had Katie sit on the bench outside the courtroom. When Douglas Smith announced he was calling Katie as a witness Robert Carrow stood up and told Judge Bennett of Katie's attempts to collect her witness fees, whereupon Judge Bennett ruled, as he was required to do by law, that Douglas Smith's refusal to pay the witness fees meant she could not be compelled to testify as a witness. As soon as he had made this ruling Douglas Smith made a rush to the courtroom door with Robert Carrow in hot pursuit. Throwing the door open, Douglas Smith told Katie to come into the courtroom, upon which Robert Carrow ordered her to stay where she was, outside the courtroom. At this juncture Judge Bennett ordered both Douglas Smith and Robert Carrow to get back in and sit down. The hearing continued without Katie's testimony and with metaphorical egg on Douglas Smith's face. Subsequently Douglas Smith never got a single cent of the $18,000 and was later ordered by another court to pay Katie's witness fees.

**Order shortening time**

While living in Sacramento with Katie, Douglas Smith would put me on notice that he would be seeking a legal procedure which is known as an Order Shortening Time. This procedure did not require the payment of any court fee or court time, it simply meant he had to give me four hours' verbal notice that he would be applying to a judge to file papers with the court for an expedited hearing on any given matter. He would put me on notice time and time again, giving me no choice but to drive to Napa to see what he would be filing with the court and, if applicable, oppose either what he was requesting or the 'shortened time' he was requesting. This was not only a flagrant abuse of process but also pure, unadulterated harassment, but because there was no record of the notice given, it was impossible to prove what he was doing.

## The Family Court Services decide that a psychological evaluation of all concerned would be of use

I thought this was a great idea. Now, perhaps, they would get some insight into Barbara's true character. I was given the name of a supposedly neutral Napa private psychologist who would do the evaluation. She would invite Barbara and me to take a psychological test known as the MMM Test which required the strictest conditions, i.e. a sealed room with nobody but the person being tested present, after which the completed test papers would be sent off for analysis. It was also agreed that Graham Jnr would be interviewed independently. To cover my side of the cost Katie paid her bill with a cashier's cheque. I sat in the sealed room and completed the test. Barbara, meanwhile, was handed the test papers and told to bring them back the next week, and it also turned out that my son was interviewed in a room with his mother in the next room with the door open. The psychologist turned out to be a friend of Douglas Smith.

A copy of Katie's cashier's cheque was delivered to Douglas Smith, who was concerned about the extent to which she was funding me. The whole exercise was a charade in itself. Moreover, the results of the process were totally skewed as this unprofessional practitioner had promised Douglas Smith and Barbara they would get the report they wanted. These were sufficient for a judge, on a Friday, based on an Order Shortening Time, to stop my access. Then, upon an emergency application before the same judge on the Monday, these same results required him to rule that the psychologist's report was so seriously flawed it was inadmissible. The order denying me access was reversed with immediate effect, but, apart from all the anguish this caused, we lost the money we had paid to her, which we could ill afford to do.

## A brainwave

On the court file there are hundreds of documents covering over one hundred and fifty court appearances or attempts at getting a court hearing over a period of six years. During this time the files were passed from judge to judge with not one of them taking the trouble to get to the root of the underlying problem: Barbara herself. Because we were just not getting any meaningful court time, John Rothschild and I decided to try and find a way round it by getting someone totally objective to look at the plethora of allegations that Barbara and Douglas Smith had been making to the courts, as a consequence of which we were always, metaphorically speaking, putting out fires. What we did was to confront this situation head-on and file an application with the court listing all the allegations Barbara and Douglas Smith had made. We requested that an attorney be appointed to represent my son and that the matter be referred back to Napa County Family Court Services. Superior Court Judge Ron Young granted our request and a local lawyer, Terence Robertson, became the attorney representing Graham Jnr. Fortunately for me, Barbara's modus operandi never changed and she started to mess him around just as she did Napa County Family Court Services, agreeing to one thing one minute and doing the opposite the next. Terry Robertson set himself the task of investigating all Barbara's allegations and subsequently, after a meeting he had with Barbara and Douglas Smith, he came to the conclusion they were fabricated.

At about the same time, Napa County Family Court Services produced a damning report in which they recommended an immediate change of custody to me. However, we had a setback here: the case worker who wrote the report had reverted to private practice and now, as a private business, she demanded a hefty fee for the required back-up oral testimony. This I could not afford, but without it her written report was worthless. However, it was pointed out to me that, even had I been able to rustle up the money to pay her fee, the former Napa County Family Court Services officer could be impeachable, i.e. her testimony could be shown to be motivated by my paying her money. Consequently, we had to fall back on the support of the Attorney for Child, Terry Robertson, and rely on the fact that he would proceed on his recommendation to the court that there be an immediate change of custody to me. He had reached the conclusion that Barbara had not only fabricated the allegations but that if she retained custody there was no way she would ever allow me access.

We had a three-week hearing set down to start on 11 April 1991, and the Attorney for Child was going to recommend an immediate change of physical custody to me, which would have meant almost certain victory. So nearly six years after the abduction, Barbara, represented by a lawyer, agreed to a twenty-seven-page joint custody agreement that pinned her down on every aspect of my rights, and stated on the transcript and in a written Order of the Court, that neither she nor our son had ever been physically, emotionally or financially abused by me; that I had never neglected him; and that her claims that I intended to abduct him were without foundation. In simple terms, Barbara admitted that what she had been telling both the San Francisco and Napa Superior Courts was a pack of lies, from start to finish.

Finally vindicated, I nonetheless had to conclude it was not in my son's interest to be uprooted from living with Barbara in Napa County and be moved eighty miles to Sacramento where I was living with Katie. It was a difficult situation as I was broke and did not own so much as a stick of furniture, and if I uprooted him I could not guarantee him a stable home. Asking Katie to locate to Napa was not an option. So Graham Jnr stayed with his mother and, for a while at least, relations were unproblematic and access proceeded without trouble.

In all those years that my custody dispute had been at the Napa Superior Court, the actual totalled-up court time was only just over seven hours. Although there had been dozens of applications to the court and dozens and dozens of appearances, there had never been a proper full hearing. Inevitably, I came across to the local judges as some sort of madman fighting windmills, so even though I had got the custody case out of the way, there was bad blood between the local judges and me.

## A disappointment

During the course of the supervised access debacle I was befriended by the pastor of the Baptist Church in Marin County. He had assisted in doing supervised visitation, let me sleep on his couch and lent me money to buy food and rent the apartment in Napa. At a later stage, when I was living with Katie, at some point in a conversation with him and his wife, I mentioned that I did not intend to marry her. On more than one occasion Katie and I had in fact been up to Reno, Nevada, to get married, but although Katie was beautiful, intelligent and loyal, I could not go through with it. My plan was to get things sorted so I could get out of the clutches of California rather than deeper in, and as Katie was a lot younger than me I did not buy her argument that although she wanted marriage she did not want more children.

One day this pastor told me he had bought a plot of land in Lake Tahoe, California, to build a holiday home and would I help him build it. He said he would pay me, but the offer of payment I declined as he had helped me when I needed it. Instead I asked him that Katie and our children would be able to use the holiday home once it was built, and he agreed. So when I was not making Monday morning court appearances in Napa, after church on the Sunday he would drive north to pick me up at Katie's home in Sacramento and we would drive north to Lake Tahoe, returning each Wednesday. We started the project at the beginning of winter, when the snow at Lake Tahoe could reach drifts of ten feet or more, and we built this house from scratch. The working and sleeping conditions were atrocious, but after eight months the house was finished; it was magnificent, warm, snug, and a great investment for the pastor and his wife.

Things went quiet, and after a while I phoned the pastor to ask if Katie and the kids could use the Lake Tahoe holiday home as had been agreed. I was stunned to be told that he had discussed things with his wife, and as my girlfriend and I were not married they did not think, as members of the church, it would be right for us to stay there. I pointed out that he knew why I did not intend to marry her and suggested other options such as Katie and I agreeing not to sleep in the same bed, or that just she and the children stay there. All of these suggestions were rejected and neither Katie nor I nor any of our children ever got a holiday there.

# ANN AND LOUISE

## Chapter 21

O nce we had sorted out my access to Graham Jnr, on 11 April 1991, Katie and I had to try and figure out what was going on with my daughters, now aged nineteen. Throughout this entire time I had tried my utmost to maintain contact with Ann and Louise, and had been thwarted at every turn by my first wife, Jane, and by some of her family. All I knew at this point was that they were living in the Canary Isles. Katie and I decided it would be good to take Graham Jnr on a trip there so he could meet with his half-sisters. To do this we needed a court order. According to two statements Barbara made to the Napa Superior Court—because as usual she opposed anything over and above the court-ordered access—my daughters had been adopted by their stepfather, and Ann had died, so we had no reason to go. Order refused.

Alarmed, Katie and I took a chance. Leaving Graham Jnr behind, Katie took out another credit card loan and paid for a two-week round trip to the island where we thought Jane was living, and rented a one-bedroom holiday let.

When we got to the island, it was not difficult to find all three of them. Mercifully, Ann was alive—Barbara's statement to the court had been another wilful lie. But what we found was every father's nightmare. Jane had remarried, but Ann and Louise's stepfather had left her for another woman, and their business, a bar, had failed. I think it right to say that while Ann was thrilled to see me, Louise was less so. And certainly none of them was overjoyed at me discovering how their lives were going: Jane drinking heavily and the girls supplying her habit with money from their jobs. I was horrified to see a large scar on Louise's arm; I discovered she had just come out of hospital having nearly lost her life when her drunk mother had kicked a glass door onto her.

Although it was now almost thirteen years since I had left Jane, one evening during one of our many visits, she turned to me in the presence of Katie and stated, "I will never forgive you for leaving me." Two wives, two women, using my children to get back at me.

Katie was unflinching in her efforts to figure out how to resolve the mess these three were in. She travelled miles every day, going from meeting to meeting, trying to find a solution. The best we could come up with was to suggest to Ann and Louise that we enrol them into the education system in California. The two girls seemed to agree to this, but it was with very heavy and worried hearts that Katie and I returned home. Katie went round in circles to get the girls into the education system, but when she succeeded, Jane told her that the girls would not be coming after all. There are no words that come even close to describing this loss.

# THE LEGAL MALPRACTICE LAWSUIT

## Chapter 22

There came a time when I had to sue Urie Walsh on account of all the financial losses he had caused me. But he was not about to give up without a fight and he hired California's premier legal malpractice defence firm to defend him.

In the litigation process in the United States you are allowed to conduct what is known as 'discovery'. This is a procedure where either side in the litigation process can request information from the other side. This is either by written questions called 'interrogatories', which have to be answered under the penalty of perjury, or 'sworn testimony' via what is known as a 'deposition', where a court reporter (stenographer) is present. Answers to questions are also given under the penalty of perjury. All of this can be used at the time of trial to impeach or confirm the written or oral testimony of the person of whom the questions were asked.

Long and Levitt devoted more than adequate resources and lawyers to his defence while digging deep into his legal malpractice insurance defence policy to pay their fees. All the while Urie Walsh was expending this money on his defence, I was flat broke. It took deposition after deposition, written interrogatory after written interrogatory, and many 'motions to compel' (application to the court to force the answering of a question) for Urie Walsh to admit that I had *not* bounced a cheque on him and that there had been no hearing of the first marriage settlement agreement. He only answered the final questions in the final motion to compel after the discovery judge told him that he would not be leaving the courtroom until he produced answers. So after depleting hundreds of thousands of dollars from his legal malpractice insurance policy, we were ready to go to trial. Once again, however, due to Urie Walsh's duplicity, things were not going to be as simple as that.

As the trial date loomed, a mandatory settlement conference, as required under Californian law, was set in the chambers of a Superior Court Judge. Lawyers from both sides were required to state their respective positions to see if there could be a resolution to the lawsuit so as to save the time and expense of a trial. This resulted in Urie Walsh's duplicity coming to light again.

The next day, as we were standing in the corridors of the San Francisco Superior Court waiting to pick a jury for the trial, Urie Walsh's lawyer approached Robert Carrow to tell him that the previous night Walsh had found some 'critical' papers (actually his handwritten notes) pertaining to his representation of me and wanted to introduce them into evidence. In the course of the pretrial litigation he had sworn time and time again he did not have these papers, stubbornly maintaining this position in his responses to written interrogatories and depositions and requests for production of the documents, even under the penalty of perjury. Now he was admitting these papers existed. This was simply because, after hearing Robert Carrow set out our case in the settlement conference, he thought they might help his own case. We now got into the blame game whereby Urie Walsh's excuse was that he thought his lawyers had them. The upshot of all this was that the trial date had to be vacated and the trial discontinued as Robert Carrow would have to take yet another deposition from Urie Walsh and the partners of his legal malpractice defence firm to find out who had these 'critical' papers and how many there were. As it turned out, a subsequent review of all these papers made Urie Walsh's level of legal malpractice easier to prove, so in fact he had shot himself in the foot.

The big problem Urie Walsh had in defending himself in the legal malpractice action was that one of my causes of action against him was the requirement to advise me to get independent legal advice, which he had failed to do. As you will recall, I had met Urie Walsh in his office at 10am on a Sunday and he had given me a Retainer Agreement secured by a Deed of Trust and Promissory Note and told me to come back at 9am the following day. As I had lived in California for only a few months and had never owned property there before, I had never heard of a Deed of Trust or Promissory Note, let alone knew what power it would give him.

The California Rules of Professional Conduct provide that:

*A member shall not enter into a business transaction with a client; or knowingly acquire an ownership, possessory, security, or other pecuniary interest adverse to a client, unless each of the following requirements is satisfied: (A) The transaction or acquisition and its terms are fair and reasonable to the client and are fully disclosed and transmitted in writing to the client in a manner which should reasonably have been understood by the client; and (B) The client is advised in writing that the client may seek the advice of an independent lawyer of the client's choice and is given a reasonable opportunity to seek that advice; and (C) The client thereafter consents in writing to the terms of the transaction or the terms of the acquisition.*

Now clutching at straws, Walsh needed to find a way, however tenuous, to try and convince a jury that he had in fact complied with Rule 3-300 section (B), even though he had not. Desperately trying to defend the indefensible, Urie Walsh's conduct sank to a new low level, which Robert Carrow and I did not find out about until later in the first day of the trial. He and his team of lawyers had already come up with a devious plot.

You may recall how, when I had first needed a lawyer for my divorce proceedings, nine years previously, Urie Walsh had been recommended to me by a lawyer named Michael Friedman whom I had met fifteen years previously when he was dating a lodger at my mother's home in England. In those subsequent fifteen years Michael Friedman had never written or spoken to my mother, or indeed any other members of my family (so in no way could he be described as a friend of the family).

Monday, 4 January 1993, was the date set for the start of my legal malpractice action at the San Francisco Superior Court. On that same day, my mother in England had, quite out of the blue, two surprise visitors to her home—none other than Michael Friedman and his office manager/secretary, who 'just happened' to be in

England on business. It was now twenty-four years since Michael Friedman had first met my mother and in the meantime had had no contact with her whatsoever. My mother did not have a clue about the San Francisco malpractice action or that it had commenced, let alone have any idea what Michael Friedman and his office secretary were up to, so the three spent an enjoyable day together and all sorts of information was disclosed.

What Robert Carrow and I later surmised was that Michael Friedman and his office secretary would immediately return to California and be called as witnesses on behalf of Urie Walsh in an attempt to show the court that he (Michael Friedman) was a family friend and that I could have sought his advice as to the Deed of Trust and Promissory Note. Inevitably, my own lawyer Robert Carrow would have been sideswiped by this revelation as he would not have known how to rebut the implied level of the relationship between my mother and Michael Friedman, which of course in real terms was zero. Had their plan worked, Michael Friedman and his office secretary would have made compelling witnesses for Urie Walsh, i.e. they would say I could have turned to Michael Friedman as a family friend for advice on the Deed of Trust and Promissory Note.

This scheming shows how desperate Urie Walsh was. Even had it met with success, there would still have been the question of Urie Walsh handing me the Deed of Trust and Promissory Note at 10am on a Sunday morning and telling me to bring it back the next morning at 9am. Not only would it have been difficult to find Michael Friedman at such an out-of-hours time, there was also the question as to whether I could have even located him. The plan fell apart as I happened to ring my mother that day and her first words were, "Guess who's been to see me—Michael Friedman—we had a lovely day . . ." The trial was in any case set aside on account of the missing 'papers'.

Not only was the trial discontinued, but the never-ending stress and tension and vacillation, not only of the trial but the preceding years, had another consequence: it was just too much for Katie. With all the money going towards the enormous litigation costs in my legal malpractice suit against Urie Walsh—expenditure that was both relentless and needless—Katie, her children and I had been living at near-subsistence level. Often we were so broke we could not keep the air conditioning on in the baking Sacramento summers. To keep cool we had to resort to the local Godfather's Pizza place where they did two large pizzas and all the Coca Cola you could drink for $9.99. So in the evenings and at weekends when we were not working on the Cook v. Cook case, we would all sit in Godfather's Pizza playing cards. If I had a dollar for every time we had to pawn our video camera just to keep going, and the times I would be at the phone company's office in Sacramento paying the phone bill at the last moment so as not to be cut off, I would have a binful of money. A sad occasion was when Katie and the children and I had to sit up one Sunday and watch our cat die as the only veterinarian open that day would not treat her unless we paid in cash, and would not even take the video camera as security.

One day I was driving out of Napa heading for Sacramento when I was rear-ended by another motorist. To my total surprise, when I took all the relevant forms into the car insurance company, without prompting I was offered $3,500 in compensation for any possible physical injuries. Later I discovered that had I consulted a lawyer in this matter the remuneration would have been at least $20,000. Regardless, it was a gift from heaven and I will always remember the joy in Katie's face when I turned up with the settlement cheque, which went a long way to easing our financial plight at the time.

It is to Katie's credit that never once did she throw in my or my son's face anything about the immense financial and personal damage all this was causing her and her children. But the accumulative stress gradually led to the breakdown of our relationship. We had assumed Urie Walsh would do the decent thing and settle the lawsuit so that we could move on. Alas, no. Consequently, from here on my relationship with Katie spiralled downwards and over the following months led to a breakdown. The best we could do was to remain friends. But it meant I was on my own again.

Robert Carrow now had to go back to square one and take Urie Walsh's deposition as to where and who had the missing 'critical' papers. Urie Walsh said his lawyers had them, so Robert Carrow started to take depositions from his lawyers, who came up with one convoluted theory after another as to where the papers were. All of this was indirectly and directly costing me money as Urie Walsh's lawyers' fees were coming off the declining balance of his insurance cover. We were set a new trial date, some months later, and as part of the defence Urie Walsh and his lawyers requested a bifurcated trial on the statute of limitations issue, based on whether my lawsuit was time-barred. This was a last-ditch defence by Urie Walsh and his lawyers to try and get my lawsuit thrown out on grounds that the statute of limitations had expired, which would prevent the case coming before a jury.

At this hearing, Robert Carrow did an absolutely magnificent job up against the phalanx of legal malpractice defence lawyers representing Urie Walsh, and there I was, in the witness stand day after day, with his team scrutinising every word I said to see if 'I knew or should have known' what Urie Walsh had done before the statute of limitations ran out. As I was being cross-examined, any word I said could have tripped me up and as a consequence my lawsuit would have been over.

In answer to one particular question, I said I had 'fobbed Urie Walsh off', at which his lawyers asked for a short adjournment. They all zoomed out of the courtroom, including Robert Carrow; they were off to the law library to see what the definition of 'fobbed' was. The judge ordered me to remain in the witness box. When the lawyers returned with their photocopies of the dictionary definitions, the judge turned to me and asked what dictionary I personally used, to which I replied 'Webster's 9th Collegiate'. The judge asked me to tell him what I meant by the use of the word 'fobbed', to which I replied that dealing with Urie Walsh was like being a child again, dealing with a bully in the school playground: you would tell the bully what he wanted to hear so as to get away from him. I was in the clear and the judge ordered that matters move on.

On every point raised by the defence, Robert Carrow prevailed, and to such an extent that at one time, from where I was sitting in the witness stand, I could see Urie Walsh come from the back of the court and thump his lead lawyer in the back, telling him to "get up there and start fucking winning." I was stunned. Then the issue of the missing papers came up, with Urie Walsh blaming his lawyers for not producing them earlier. At this point the judge declared a mistrial because he believed someone was lying, either Urie Walsh or his lawyers, and as he did not know who, it would affect his judgment.

After all this waste of money, with Urie Walsh using up his insurance cover on a desperate defence of his actions, I suggested to Robert Carrow that he contact the loss adjuster for Urie Walsh's insurance company and see if he could settle the lawsuit with the insurance company direct. Otherwise Urie Walsh would simply go on depleting whatever money was left on the policy. A meeting was arranged and the insurance company settled the legal malpractice case over Urie Walsh's head—still with no admission by him of liability.

At the settlement conference both Robert Carrow and I were astonished at the judge's statement that he had known Urie Walsh for years and was surprised that something like this had not happened before, i.e. Urie Walsh being sued for legal malpractice.

What was most interesting about my legal malpractice case was that neither Walsh's lawyers nor Robert Carrow called the one person you would think to be the star witness: Barbara. Urie Walsh had once described her, when representing me in the divorce proceedings, as a prolific and plausible liar. The simple fact was that Barbara was such a wild card and liar that neither side dared call her as a witness, as whatever testimony she produced could have been a time bomb for either side as she would simply make things up. The very first rule of law in the courtroom is: you never call a witness or ask a question unless you know what they are going to say . . .

We were now into July of 1993. I was back staying at a cheap motel again in Mill Valley, along with Graham Jnr under the terms of my joint custody order. After Robert Carrow had received the settlement cheque, Graham Jnr and I sat in the foyer of his offices while he deducted his outstanding fees. He then calculated the cost of all the undertakings he had given to the rest of the legal team so he could pay their fees before paying me. I ended up with a mere fraction of what I was previously worth, but at least I was vindicated.

# AN IDYLLIC INTERLUDE

## Chapter 23

In anticipation of getting the settlement money from Urie Walsh's insurance carrier I had done a lot of pre-planning, not the least of which was paying back the friend who had fronted my motel bill, arranging to pay for a second-hand Volkswagen convertible, buying a mobile phone and making all the necessary preparations so Graham Jnr and I could be gone for the summer. After Robert Carrow had paid off all my lawyer creditors we drew from him two trustee's cheques drawn on a small local bank, one for the car and one for cash. Apart from money I wanted to give to Katie, the rest would be spending money for our summer trip. As long as I got Graham Jnr back to Barbara two weeks before school started for the autumn term in Napa, the holiday would last all summer long.

At the bank it was a late Friday afternoon before we got there and they did not have enough cash on hand to pay the two cheques I presented. As a cheque in California is payable on demand, we had to wait for the bank to order up the cash from the Federal Reserve in San Francisco and the armoured car to deliver it! Having paid for the car we went to the local camping shop to buy all the gear we would need for the summer, then headed north to Sacramento to Katie's home. I wish I could have been present to see the look on her and her children's faces when Graham Jnr went into the living room and emptied the contents of a shoe box stuffed with $100 bills onto the living room floor as our way of saying thank you.

Now my son and I were free to be gone all summer, driving where we wanted and spending what we wanted for two whole months. We decided to head on north of Sacramento and go back to

Coeur d'Alene, Idaho, to see if we could look up the old friends we had met the year before. Then we headed north to Montana, east to the Dakotas, south to Nebraska, west to Missouri, south to Arkansas and Louisiana, and west to Texas.

Graham Jnr was eleven at the time and was doing the navigating using a large map book. We knew Texas was big, but after days of driving we never seemed to get any closer to where we wanted to go—the birthplace of the greatest Texan ever born in Lubbock, Buddy Holly. After a further few puzzling days I discovered that two pages of the atlas were stuck together! Eventually reaching Texas we then went on to New Mexico and Arizona. By now we were getting fed up with camping so in Mesa we bought a large motor home and towed the Volkswagen convertible back to Napa. The other reason for the motor home was that I did not have any accommodation to go back to and was not sure where I was going to live.

This was an idyllic, carefree summer covering thousands of miles, seeing all sorts of fabulous places such as Elvis Presley's former home, Graceland, in Memphis, plus the Lorraine Motel where Martin Luther King had been assassinated, and the National Civil Rights Museum, a very powerful place to visit. We witnessed amazing things like the geysers at Yellowstone National Park and tornados in the Dakotas. We toured New Orleans and visited the Grand Canyon, doing all the things that as father and son we might have done before had it not been for those eight years of solid, unrelenting litigation.

When Graham Jnr and I returned to Napa with the motor home, I rented a permanent parking space on a motor park on the outskirts of Napa. No sooner had we settled into our allotted space than an amazing thing happened. As we were sitting outside the motor home, who should pull up, dressed in the last handmade dress I had bought her eight years earlier just before the abduction and looking at her very, very best? It was Barbara. This was the selfsame woman who along with everything else she had done in all those years always refused to utter so much as one word to me or acknowledge me as a human being. She asked if she could sit down, asked Graham Jnr to fetch her a beer and me for a cigarette. Our jaws were dropped in utter astonishment. With tears in her eyes she told me that she had read the *San Francisco Examiner* article about my successful lawsuit against Urie Walsh which had been published some months earlier. She then stated, in reference to the bounced cheque, "So you were telling the truth all along", to which I replied, "Yes, Barbara, I told you I had never bounced a cheque on Walsh."

The truth of the matter was, Barbara smelled money. Although she had no idea how much money I might have after the Urie Walsh lawsuit was settled, it was worth pursuing, and in her eyes the 'small' matter of what she had been up to for eight years could be simply swept away; in her own world we would let the last eight years disappear into history and be forgotten. That was Barbara for you.

After her beer and cigarette Barbara went off in the Dodge Omni car, which was the same car whose settlement value Urie Walsh had promised to wipe off his bill, the car that had caused all the confusion back in January 1985. Indirectly, that car must have been one of the most expensive ever produced.

# WINSTON'S

## Chapter 24

Eventually it became apparent that remaining in the motor home was no longer viable as I wanted somewhere permanent and more suitable for Graham Jnr to stay. I sold it and rented a new condominium in a complex near to where Barbara lived and furnished it accordingly. Barbara's opinion of me had been affected by her realisation that I had been telling the truth all along about Urie Walsh, and on account of that she was much less hostile. In fact we used to sit next to each other at our son's school soccer games.

With my private life impeccable, I was now living in Napa, jointly raising my son with Barbara and trying to open a 7,000 square foot, upmarket British/Irish brew pub called Winston's. In all those years since my son had been abducted from England I had not been able to exercise my skills as an entrepreneur. I had had to survive as an employee, which was particularly painful for me as I was not accustomed to working for other people. Previously I had always needed and risen to the stimulus of a challenge, and was enormously self-driven. Naturally, now I had some funds once more, I wanted to build a business again and, hopefully, a fortune.

I decided to invest the remainder of the money left over from the settlement of my lawsuit against Urie Walsh in creating a brew pub. Brew pubs were very fashionable at the time. They were licensed premises where the beer is brewed on-site and the huge brass and copper brewing vats and brewing equipment were an integral part of the process, which customers could view.

My vision was huge, as you will see from the following business plan.

# EXECUTIVE SUMMARY

## PROJECT

To create an upscale authentic British/Irish Brew Pub in the Napa Town Centre Mall, which will be the prototype for three other pubs to be developed in Sacramento, San Jose and the Bay Area. The pubs will be known as Winston's, and the theme will be the life and times of Sir Winston Spencer Churchill (1874-1965). The 4,800-square-foot interior will replicate a British/Irish pub circa 1890. Winston's will operate as an informal social club consisting of two bars, pool room, conference room, gift shop and international newspaper stand. Winston's is purchasing an On Sale General Eating Place License Type 47, which will authorize the sale of all alcoholic beverages on the premises and the sale of packaged beer and wine off the premises. There will be a full range of beers, liquor, wines and authentic pub food plus a "lite" menu. In keeping with Winston's marketing strategy, additional services will be offered to clients such as a meeting room with desktop publishing facilities. Opening date is anticipated to be March 1995.

## MARKETING

Winston's will be a seven-days-a-week venue with a social heart—a business that will cater to the whole community. The Brew Pub is being promoted as a meeting and destination site to business organizations, civic and community groups, wedding and party planners, tour operators, and social clubs.

Winston's will create an ambience designed to take its patrons back in time and, to this end, is importing original Cotswold stone for the interior walls and flagstones for the floors. The Cotswold stone is from a quarry which has been in existence since the Roman occupation of Britain. The quarry supplied the Oxford University (Merton College, c.1300; New College, c.1400; University College, c.1600); Blenheim Palace, the birthplace of Churchill; and the American Museum in Bath, the site of Churchill's first political speech in 1897. The flagstones, circa 1805, are from Shires Mill, Yorkshire, England. The pub will have fireplaces, wooden beams, authentic bric-a-brac, memorabilia, and antiques.

Winston's attention to historical detail is being well-received. Already, on both sides of the Atlantic, more than two dozen news stories have appeared on radio and TV and in local and international publications—from the *Napa County Record* to the *Financial Times of London.* On August 2, 1994, the BBC filmed and broadcast the cutting of stone in the quarry and its loading on the truck to begin its journey to Napa. There have been favorable remarks about Winston's by Winston Churchill, MP, the grandson of Sir Winston Churchill.

Lake, Marin, Napa, SF and Sonoma Co. Bar Association Members...

# You're In Good Company.

(YOUR NAME)

John Smith, Esq.
ATTORNEY AT LAW

**A** s an attorney practicing in Lake, Marin, Napa, San Francisco, and/or Sonoma Counties, you are entitled to a Winston's charge card.

• 5% discount on all non-alcoholic purchases.
• A further 5% discount on all non-alcoholic purchases between 9:30am to 11:30am and 2pm to 3:30pm, Monday through Friday.
• Free use of the meeting room, library, and Lexus terminal.

**Open**
Sun.-Fri. 8am-11pm
Sat. 8am-Midnight

**I** t's simple to apply. Please fill out the application below and send us the $25 enrollment fee, and we'll send you a personalized Winston's beer mug with your name permanently fired on the mug.

**Conditions**
• Applicants must be members of the Lake, Marin, Napa, San Francisco, and/or Sonoma County Bar Associations.
• Discounts only apply to cardholder's purchases.
• Winston's reserves the right to decline any application.
• Winston's reserves the right to discontinue the Monday through Friday special hours discounts.

**Phone:**
(707) 254-1083/4/5

**Fax:**
(707) 254-1086

# WINSTON'S
*Authentic British / Irish Brew Pubs*

Name: _____

Company: _____

Address: _____

_____

Telephone #: _____

Fax #: _____

Please mail with $25 to Winston's Authentic British/Irish Brew Pubs. P.O Box 5417 • Napa CA 94581

# ANOTHER KAFKAESQUE NIGHTMARE

## Chapter 25

While I was trying to get my new business organised I was introduced to a woman called Tess Francis by the owner/editor of a tabloid newspaper called *The Napa Sentinel.* Her office was next door to that of the newspaper and I had seen her on one of my visits to talk to the editor.

Tess Francis was attractive and we enjoyed a satisfying physical relationship, but after a very short period of time, just a few weeks, I decided to end our relationship as it became increasingly clear to me that she was a metaphoric time bomb waiting to go off. I had only recently prevailed in my custody action and was handling things with care in that direction. At the same time I was concentrating on the business of opening my British/Irish brew pub, and needed Tess Francis and her plethora of problems like a hole in the head.

Here was a woman who had falsified her job application upon which she had gained employment and daily feared getting caught; who displayed irrational anger to a previous boyfriend who she claimed had rejected her; was fiddling her business expenses and time sheets; and who never drove her truck without resorting to constant horn-blowing and V finger signs. She loathed and detested her father who she claimed had molested her, and her insecurity and paranoia even extended to her believing I had once been married to a woman whose only offence was to lend me a vacation home. I had bought her a computer so she could catch up at home with the tasks she could not do at work, but this turned out to be a waste of time as all she wanted to do was watch television.

The final straw came over something totally inconsequential: a carton of milk. We had been at Tess Francis's parents' home over the

Christmas period and she had walked to her father's fridge and drunk directly from the carton of milk there. This set off a tirade between the two of them which was not only painful to watch, but, witnessing all the enmity between them, ruined my Christmas. I realised I was walking into a set of family problems I could well do without. When we returned home I tried to reason with Tess, asking her if she could not see things from her father's perspective. After all, he was her father, it was his home and most people did not like people directly drinking from milk cartons. Off she went again with a tirade about her father; the hatred she displayed was simply awful to see.

I ended the relationship and expected to move on with my life, my two major concerns being to raise my son and open my pub. I did everything by the book, having learned a lot from my former custody proceedings, and the last thing I wanted was to get caught up in the Napa County court system again. I have looked back on the way I ended the relationship with Tess Francis and maybe I could have done things more gently. Anyway, I found myself in a hornet's nest.

## *The Napa Sentinel*

There was in existence a free tabloid newspaper, *The Napa Sentinel*, edited by Harry Martin, which was circulated throughout Napa. It published vile and often false stories about the citizens of Napa. Its editor hid behind the freedom of speech provisions as outlined in the US Constitution, or the fact that the paper was immune from lawsuits, using the defence that *The Napa Sentinel* was writing about public figures about whom the general populace had 'a right to know'. If you were unfortunate enough to cross Harry Martin, he would use his newspaper in an effort to destroy you. He appeared to derive maximum enjoyment from ruining people's lives, and was also notorious for writing about and expounding the most bizarre conspiracy theories.

At the time this part of the story occurred, Mr Martin's former business partner was serving seventeen years in a federal penitentiary for operating a Ponzi scheme (a criminal enterprise whereby an investor borrows from another investor, promising high returns, to pay off yet another investor and so on), and his lawyer went to jail for assaulting a teenager. Not the most salubrious of associates.

The manner in which this tabloid operated was as sordid as it could possibly get. One of Harry Martin's many openly professed and notorious claims to fame was his boast that a court had ruled that he had been in breach of the regulations for publishing legal notices by falsifying the requirements for their publication. This was how Harry Martin conducted himself and his newspaper. In the past he had always published highly favourable articles about me personally, but then I fell foul of him. My fall from popularity resulted when I personally questioned his sanity about how he operated his tabloid.

## The temporary restraining order

I had written to Tess Francis twice, explaining why I had ended the relationship, requesting her not to contact me and asking for the return of some personal property owned by me. Within weeks she had applied to the courts for a temporary restraining order. A restraining order can only be applied for when there is a fear of violence, but even though our relationship had ended she had come to my home on two occasions, unescorted, which clearly shows she did not fear for her safety. However, as we all know, it's impossible to disprove a negative. In support of her application she used a rambling, two-page declaration containing a plethora of false and irrelevant allegations, none of which even remotely alleged any violence or threats by me to her. This was a counter strike by her, prompted by Harry Martin, who later gloated to me that it was he who had put her up to it. She was represented by a local lawyer, Lynne Young, who was later disbarred by the State Bar of California for dishonesty on unrelated matters.

It was a typical Napa County Consolidated Courts' shambles. When the day came for the hearing, no proper time had been allocated. Even if there had been, I was back to square one as I would have been in front of one of the local judges who had been involved in my long-running dispute with Barbara, so we would have had all that baggage to get past. I had another problem insofar as my lawyer Robert Carrow had an appearance to make at a court hearing in another county at the new time set for my own hearing. As well as not being able to be present, he had been having problems within his family and, unusually, he was not functioning as optimally as he normally did. Between the two of them—he and Barbara Corotto—I was pressurised into agreeing to a mutual restraining order. To this day Barbara Corotto regrets the pressure she put me under to enter into this order, although opposing it would have been a pointless exercise as judges on the whole will sign a restraining order to protect themselves. Naturally, none of us could have imagined in our wildest dreams that we were giving Tess Francis the ultimate weapon to exact her vengeance on me for rejecting her.

Even though, as a condition of my agreeing to the mutual restraining order, Tess Francis withdrew her false and irrelevant allegations, the judge had not followed his statutory duty and advised me that any violations to the restraining order—real or alleged— would be subject to criminal proceedings as opposed to civil contempt proceedings, and this later resulted in a big problem for me.

No sooner had the mutual restraining order been entered into the court record, than off went Tess Francis, with the support of Harry Martin and his tabloid, to file a series of false police reports containing bizarre and unsubstantiated allegations which were many and varied. Her intent was to destroy my chances of opening my pub.

## Motion to vacate the restraining order

Line by line Robert Carrow and I had taken apart the declaration filed by Tess Francis in support of her temporary restraining order, which had become the mutual restraining order. By her own actions in trying to cover her tracks, and the use of a private investigator, we showed conclusively that every single statement sworn by her was a wilful lie. As a result we went along standard procedure and filed an application with the court to vacate the mutual restraining order. This was not because I wanted any contact with Tess Francis but because I objected to her false statements appearing on the public record.

It was unfortunate for me that the judge designated to hear the matter was Judge Bennett. He had not only issued some of the bizarre orders in my custody action, but also harboured a grudge because I had reported his friend Judge Snowden to the Commission on Judicial Performance for the way he had conducted himself when holding the hearing on the temporary restraining order. He was also aggrieved because one of his previous judgments against me in my custody action came to nothing when Barbara and Douglas Smith said they would support me in my appeal against his order.

Judge Bennett had the unenviable reputation of shooting from the hip and my chances of ever getting a fair hearing before him were about as remote as my chances of marrying the Queen of England. True to form, Judge Bennett denied my motion, awarded attorney fees against me—more than was requested by Tess Francis and her lawyer, Michael Calhoun—and more importantly, removed from the court file (public record) two declarations that had been served by a professional process server on Michael Calhoun. The importance of these two declarations, the removal of which meant they were not available to the Napa County District Attorney if and when the underlying file was reviewed, was that they irrefutably proved that I could not have been guilty of two of the charges that I was accused of. If Judge Bennett had bothered to look, he would have found that Michael Calhoun had in fact responded to them, so not only had he replied, it meant there was proof on file that the declarations had been served. This specious act by Judge Bennett would have a significant effect on me in the subsequent proceedings.

The other thing this judge did not do was admonish Michael Calhoun, as he should have done, for bringing to his attention that I had reported Judge Snowden to the Commission on Judicial Performance. The disturbing factor about Judge Bennett was his unnatural preoccupation with me and that he was interfering in something that was nothing to do with him. His biased attitude cannot be better indicated than by a remarkable incident that even by his swaggering antics went beyond the pale and should have been reported to the California Commission on Judicial Performance. The incident in question involved a situation where a court reporter—stenographer—was required to be present in Judge Bennett's chambers. He ordered that a long-established and well-respected local lawyer, James V. Jones, leave Judge Bennett's chambers, go to the lawyers' offices and come back with the cash to pay the court reporter, even though that person had not requested it. This payment was none of Judge Bennett's business and the normal and absolute protocol would be for the court reporter to invoice James Jones. What Judge Bennett did was to shock James Jones to the core and send out a message to the local legal community that helping me would have consequences. The trouble is, when you report a judge in a small county like Napa you just dig yourself in deeper as the other judges will give you payback time for reporting one of their own. It is known in the legal fraternity as 'a black robe conspiracy' and there is nothing the Commission on Judicial Performance can do to protect you.

## The false police reports

There were over thirty written reports which subsequently led to ten criminal charges against me. A simple examination of these police reports will show how bogus all of this was.

### I had cut off the head of a doll and placed it on the antenna of her truck.

When this alleged act took place, Tess Francis had driven to an appointment with her lawyer Michael Calhoun at his office, which of course I would not have known, and his offices were opposite the courthouse. What possible opportunity would I have had to commit the act, had it ever happened? I later quizzed Michael Calhoun about this incident and was given another couple of curved balls— apparently they suspected me when the tyres of Harry Martin's van were slashed, but when I approached *The Napa Sentinel's* editor about this he told me I had never been suspected. Michael Calhoun also stated I was the suspect when the windows of Douglas Smith's office were blown out, but again, when I approached Douglas Smith about this he told me it had never occurred to him to think it was me.

### I had vandalized Tess Francis's boyfriend's car.

I had no idea she had a boyfriend, what he looked like, what car he drove, or even cared. Asked to produce documentation relating to any repairs resulting from this alleged incident, she could not or would not.

**A male person with lots of big hair wearing blue jeans and a blue shirt came into her office, his actions seemed strange and she thought I might have sent him.**

Tess Francis had her office next door to that of *The Napa Sentinel*. She worked for a charity that assisted people with learning disabilities, so this person could have been anyone, for any reason.

**Someone had been in her apartment, moved several items and taken a spray bottle.**

What stunned the police officer investigating this report was that she shared the large house she was living in with several other persons, all of whom had access to her room. I did not have the remotest idea where she even lived.

**I had siphoned gas out of her car.**

The only way to siphon off the gasoline was by prising open the external flap on the side of her car. She reported no damage to the flap or surrounding area.

**I had altered the fuel gauge on her car so that she would run out of gas.**

The only way to alter the fuel gauge was from the inside of the car; there was no report of damage or entry to the car, which anyway had been parked on a public street. Moreover, to alter the fuel gauge would have required removing the dashboard, and no damage was reported there either. In fact it was impossible to tamper with the fuel gauge of that particular make and model of car.

**I had wiped a burrito over her truck.**

Well, who knows if that ever really happened and if it did, what was it to do with me?

**I had vandalized hers and her parents' cars.**

Again, who knows if that ever happened? In the subsequent criminal proceedings no documentation was produced to support these allegations and no photographs were ever produced showing any damage.

**I had offered her a $500,000 bribe to dismiss the criminal charges.**

Apart from not even remotely having this sort of money or making the phone call to her, at the time this incident was alleged to have taken place I was standing in the middle of the street talking to a local lawyer; I was waiting to do a television interview about my issues with the *Napa Sentinel,* so was witnessed by the entire camera crew.

**Her shed door was found open.**

As it turned out, this shed was often left unlocked and her neighbour had access to it.

**Two persons were sitting in a car outside her home.**

If this had ever happened there was a big problem with it—the police reported that Tess Francis had moved home and there was no way I could have known where she had moved to.

**A car had followed her down the freeway for a few hundred yards, turned around and gone in another direction.**

Tess Francis was unable to give the police a description of the car or its driver, and with 28,000,000 cars on the road in the State of California, I think most rational people would accept that this type of incident occurs every day.

**I had left a strange message on her boyfriend's answering machine.**

Not only did I not know she had a boyfriend, let alone who he was, Tess Francis was unable to produce the answering machine tape.

**I had followed her into a post office.**

Tess Francis complained that she had walked into the main post office in downtown Napa and I was present, which violated the restraints on how near we were allowed to be to each other. The problem with this police report was that Ms Francis had moved her post office box (after the issuance of the mutual restraining order) from the Trancas Street post office to the downtown post office where she knew I had my post office box. Inevitably I would be in the post office line at some point when she too came in. In the police report she states the purpose of her being there was to pay for her new post office box.

**I had violated the mutual restraining order one Friday afternoon as I was walking my dog in Jefferson Street in Napa.**

I was simply walking my dog to pick up my mail from the downtown post office at the end of town where I lived, the main street being miles long. Tess Francis was driving her truck in the opposite direction, namely towards me, and as we came within the number of yards we were not to go near each other (I on the pavement, remember, she on the road) she claimed I was violating the restraining order.

**I was seen looking at her truck.**

I was looking at her truck in a public car park. In fact the incident took place at the car park of the offices of *The Napa Sentinel* as naturally I wanted to see if her truck had really been vandalised, which it had not. It is interesting to note it was Harry Martin who reported this to Tess Francis.

**I was in violation of the mutual restraining order when she walked into my health club on a Saturday morning.**

I was sitting on a rowing machine on the second floor and she told the police officer she had seen my car in the health club car park. However, according to Tess Francis's befuddled logic, I was in violation of the mutual restraining order. Should I have known she would be coming to that particular health club?

**One Sunday morning I called her home, speaking with a Spanish accent.**

Apart from, obviously, having an English accent and not making the phone call, it subsequently emerged that Tess Francis had her truck up for sale so would have expected phone calls. She later stated that the alleged phone call took place on the Monday when she was in her office.

**I had constant police reports that she had been receiving phone hang-ups at work.**

Well, of course it is impossible to disprove a negative and also there was not only no proof these calls had ever been made, but by the very nature of the work she did and the type of clients she dealt with, phone hang- ups would have been part of the job. She produced a log, but when some of the alleged phone calls were made she would not have been at work. However, one of the police reports was illuminating with regard to her state of mind when she said to a police officer, "It's been seven months since I witnessed him hearing voices."

By filing this plethora of false police reports, Tess Francis was violating the same mutual restraining order she sought my prosecution under. Even Barbara thought what was going on was ridiculous, as did others. One of these was my best friend, Gary, a California Highway Patrol officer. Other friends were Dr Bruce Beckler who was in charge of the local police training college; a school teacher who was living under a police change of identity (because she was a rape victim and the rapist's brother had threatened to kill her); and even Judge Champlin's secretary who was a friend of mine and who had previously stopped me in the corridor of the courtroom and told me I was being stitched up.

Thus each evening at 7pm, the local unattached females in my housing complex, together with their dogs, would congregate outside my home, and Graham Jnr and I would escort them on a dog walk through the nearby isolated countryside. Clearly the women who knew me did not believe the police reports.

Between the endless false reports and *The Napa Sentinel* articles (detailed in the next chapter), with their intrusion into my private life at every turn, I felt like a hunted animal. In sheer desperation I phoned Tess Francis's sister Jacqueline in Chicago, leaving a message on her phone answering machine pleading to be left alone. This was not in violation of any mutual restraining order, nonetheless I was subsequently criminally charged on this phone call. The false police reports continued regardless.

I went to the City of Napa Police Department to request a meeting with a senior police officer to see what they could do about this endless harassment and was told at the meeting that, although they too were sick and tired of the bogus complaints, there was nothing they could do as each report had to be followed up.

Tess Francis's mother then joined in the affray, alleging I had phoned her home in violation of the mutual restraining order. The improbable aspect here was that a) her mother was not a named party to the order; b) I had never made the phone call; and c) even if I had wanted to I could not as it was an unlisted number.

The declaration also claimed I had deposited a picture of Tess Francis's former attorney, Lynne Young, in her mailbox. Lynne Young was running for the office of District Attorney at this time, which of course meant election leaflets were being distributed.

Tess Francis's mother claimed that I had followed her vehicle for approximately three-quarters of a mile and tailgated her car. This was another false allegation as at that time I had no car in my possession, my car being up for sale forty miles away in Mill Valley. Through phone records and third-party witnesses I could prove I was at home all that day, whereas Tess's mother was not able to identify either the time, make, model or even colour of the car that allegedly tailgated her. I filed and served a declaration with the court that proved conclusively that she had lied. Unbelievably, my declaration was improperly removed from the court record by Judge Richard Bennett, and I was criminally charged, based on Tess Francis's mother's false allegation. As my declaration was filed with the clerk of the court, Judge Bennett had no legal authority to remove it. His reason was that it had not been properly served by a professional process server. Of course it had been properly served: after my experiences with the law in California I didn't take risks with the legal process.

## Chapter 26

Despite living a law-abiding life, trying to jointly raise my son, build a British/Irish brew pub and move on with my life, the false police reports and appalling articles in *The Napa Sentinel* continued, the tabloid and Tess Francis caring not at all what ends they used to achieve their objective of stopping me opening up the pub. My son was being taunted at school so much that he asked me if he could change his name.

I formed a friendship with a young lady, Kelly, who was friends with one of my Napa neighbours. *The Napa Sentinel* employed someone to circulate copies of the tabloid to my neighbours and landlord in Napa and to Kelly's ex-husband in Sacramento. This person not only photographed the inside of my home but would stand outside my house giving hand gestures as if he had a gun in his hand, but by the time the police arrived he'd have disappeared. Each time I left Napa to visit Kelly, condoms were left on my doorstep or my potted plants were knocked over.

The owner of the building where Winston's was to be located made it a condition for using the building that his best friend should be the pub's general building contractor. He was not someone I welcomed with open arms as, in the past, he openly admitted he had once been charged with threatening to kill his former wife's boyfriend and had been the subject of a six-day sanity hearing, at which time he was brought, shackled, before Judge Bennett. However, very reluctantly, I agreed.

One day he was in the same courtroom as Tess Francis—whom he had never met—and where Judge Bennett was presiding. For reasons beyond my comprehension, he approached Tess Francis in

Judge Bennett's courtroom and introduced himself as the general contractor for my brew pub, and they became friends. Of course as soon as I discovered this I terminated my relationship with him on the spot, as considering his past history it might appear that I was attempting to intimidate a witness. He then became the source of a plethora of false news stories in *The Napa Sentinel* about a cheque payment I had made to him. As a personal friend of Tess Francis he appeared on the witness list against me at my forthcoming trial, although for the life of me I did not have a clue as to his relevance to the prosecution. In fact his testimony could have only helped my defence.

It was not only this incessant harassment that made my life a misery, I also had to contend with *The Napa Sentinel*. The tabloid launched a full-scale, front page attack on me, copies of the paper being personally delivered to my neighbours in Napa. Things were so pervasive I had police knocking on my door at all hours of the night and day, and on one occasion a police officer turned up with a police dog and searched my home. It is ironic that he subsequently had to resign from the police force for harassing his girlfriend.

I applied to be a volunteer at the local hospital and was turned down because of the adverse publicity. When I became a Meals on Wheels volunteer *The Napa Sentinel* wrote an article claiming I was doing this in the hope of meeting elderly people so as to rip them off. Even when I decided to go to church to find some help with alleviating the stress I was under, the pastor of my local church ran a background check on me with Harry Martin.

What Harry Martin did not point out to *The Napa Sentinel* readers was that its sales manager, Robert Veilluex, a neighbour of mine, had developed what can best be described as a close personal relationship with Tess Francis, and it was possible to track the false police reports and *The Napa Sentinel* articles to Robert Veilluex passing on to Tess Francis any developments in either my personal or business life. When I was at the swimming pool in the complex where I was living, he was also frequently there, and if I was talking to any female tenants you could bet your bottom dollar it would be followed up with one of Tess Francis's false reports and there would be a phone call from the Napa City Police Department when I got back to my apartment. Unless you have lived in a small county such as Napa, it will be difficult to understand the fear and control that Harry Martin and his tabloid exerted over many of the residents of the county, who were terrified lest they become the centre of his attention. It was a de facto reign of terror. Add to this the scorned woman, Tess Francis, and *The Napa Sentinel's* sales manager wanting to get off with her, and the result was a no-holds-barred persecution by this toxic threesome.

Here are some examples of the headlines I had to contend with from Harry Martin and his newspaper:

## IS IT DÉJÀ VU?

This went on for five pages with sub-titles of:

'**Exclusive Report—Who Is Graham Cook?; Financing Winston's on a Shoestring; Pub Promoter Charged by DA; Pub Promoter Threatens Suit; Court Orders Him to Stand Trial for 10 Criminal Counts; Arraigned on 10 Criminal Counts; Pub Promoter Ordered by Judge to Stand Trial; Bounced Checks, Attorneys, Judges, Investigators and Women; If Guilty, Pub Promoter Could Face Deportation; He was called Nutso when his wife wanted him locked up for 72 hours at Napa State Hospital; A \$500,000 Witness Bribe? DA Will Investigate Charge; Bad Week For Cook—Winston's Collapses; Cook in a Stew; Cook Must Stand Trial, Court Rules Restraining Orders Were Valid; Would-Be British Pub Promoter Faces 8 Counts; International Question Doesn't Compute; Media World Upside Down—Cook Claims Sentinel Name, Martin Takes the Rest; Mall Owners Refute Cook. They Testify that British Pub Promoter Lied about his Business Background; Cook Attacks his Own Witnesses on Ouster; Victim Still Fears British Alien; Cook Gets Taxpayers to Pay for Attorney; Smear Campaign Launched By Alien.**

Nothing in *The Napa Sentinel* articles was sacred. It published information as to its perception of my child support payments, car payments, rent payments, garbage bill payments. It speculated about how I paid for my grocery bills, the status of Kelly's rent payments, my cell phone payments, how I paid my lawyers and the level of the salary of the person who was to be Winston's general manager. Kelly's name and address were published and readers were encouraged to write to her. The name and phone number of the Napa City Police Special Investigations Department was published, and readers were encouraged to file complaints. Even the perceived status of my dog's licence was published. They also falsely published that I had ordered the destruction of all my business records relating to the pub because the City of Napa Police Narcotics Department had served a warrant on my bank accounts.

The tabloid's lawyer, Matt Bishop, arranged a meeting between me and Harry Martin to have a free, frank and forthright discussion as to how things could be resolved. The ground rules were that anything discussed would not be publicly disseminated. I met with Harry Martin and told him I was prepared to let bygones be bygones, and proposed a way of settling things. The following week there was yet another demeaning article disseminating what had been discussed at the meeting—a gross violation of what had been agreed.

Unfortunately, the corrosive effect of all this coverage meant my chances of ever getting a fair trial in Napa County were becoming more and more remote. In fact, Tess Francis was so pleased with the exposure I was getting in *The Napa Sentinel* she left a message on my voicemail stating, "No business no pub. You really got reamed in *The Napa Sentinel!* Get a life, Babe!" This was a direct violation of the same mutual restraining order she was enforcing through the Napa DA's office, so I handed over the message tape as incontrovertible evidence of her act. Not a thing was done. Compare this with the ten charges I faced after her baseless accusations of leaving a shed door open and the like, to see the inequity of the Napa legal system.

There were many more headline articles, all equally malicious, the purpose being to try and bring me down and prevent me from getting a fair trial in Napa.

My friendship with Kelly had meanwhile developed into a deeper relationship and when I was being evicted from my rented house for not being able to afford to continue paying the rent, she suggested I should move out of the quagmire in Napa and live with her in Sacramento. Even when I was moving house, so pervasive was *The Napa Sentinel* in my life that I found a photographer from the tabloid in my home, photographing the interior.

When I moved in with Kelly the same thing happened as had happened in Napa, and copies of the tabloid were delivered to Kelly's next-door neighbours, ex-husband and landlord. So concerned was Kelly's former husband about the content of the articles that there was a flurry of legal activity, where through his lawyer he demanded that passports be surrendered and that their six-year-old child should not be left alone with me. Eventually, once he became aware of the truth of things, all was resolved and our relationship became amicable.

As well as *The Napa Sentinel* we also had to deal with the tricks of Tess Francis's lawyer, Michael Calhoun. He made an application and order for the re-issuance of the mutual restraining order, adding Tess Francis's mother to the order, even though it was time barred, that is, outside the permitted period of time to allow such an action to be brought. This did not deter Michael Calhoun. After the applicable judge signed the order, Calhoun altered the date set for the hearing on the copy sent to me—a date later than that set for the hearing, as a consequence of which, clearly through no fault of mine, I did not appear, and the order was granted.

At this point Robert Carrow and I had a brainwave: we brought an Order to Show Cause Re: Contempt, listing all the false police reports, on the basis that Tess Francis was violating my rights under the mutual restraining order. Michael Calhoun, by now both Tess Francis's and her mother's lawyer, brought an *ex parte* application, contravening every applicable local Rule of Court and California Rule of Court, with a hearing set for the next morning at 8.30am. With no moving papers served on me the court granted Calhoun's request and stayed my Order to Show Cause Re: Contempt, pending the outcome of the criminal proceeding. This was a gross violation of my inalienable right to mount a lawful defence in my pending criminal proceedings. Robert Carrow filed a motion to dismiss the criminal charges because of this egregious violation of my due process rights, but the motion was denied.

Another major problem was Judge Champlin's refusal to recuse himself (withdraw on account of personal bias). It meant I could not exercise my constitutional right to a no-jury trial because of Judge Champlin's prejudice. And *The Napa Sentinel's* unremitting front page articles, though false, made my chances of finding an impartial jury in such a small county next to impossible. As a resident alien of the United States, a conviction on such charges would likely lead to deportation proceedings, a fact of which all concerned were well aware.

Tess Francis's lawyer, Michael Calhoun (now disbarred), used to boast that I would never get a fair hearing at the Napa Superior Court, and he was right. I filed motions and declarations, took depositions, went to the City of Napa Police Department trying to get someone somewhere to figure out what Tess Francis, her mother and Harry Martin were up to. It was like banging my head against a brick wall. Even Ms Francis's former lawyer, Lynne Young (also now disbarred), told me she did not believe I was doing what was alleged of me. All this could have been avoided if the Napa County legal system had followed the applicable Rules of Court, and the law.

Later, represented by lawyers, I sued Harry Martin and *The Napa Sentinel* and was successful. I could get no money from him, but he did agree to write nothing more about me and acknowledged that he knew the stuff he had been writing about me was false. In fact, his own lawyer told me he felt sorry for me and had withdrawn from the case because he thought Harry Martin and his newspaper had gone too far.

Things caught up with Harry Martin in the end, however, as he and his wife were evicted from their home for failing to pay the rent, and he ended up in the Napa County homeless shelter, abandoned by all and sundry.

# BOGUS PROSECUTION

## Chapter 27

I was charged with ten counts of violating the mutual restraining order. Lest there be any doubt about how bogus these charges were, not once was I arrested or questioned on any of the police reports and not once did the District Attorney's Office request I be remanded in custody.

Judge Champlin was the designated judge and Robert Carrow represented me. Mr Carrow and I were both taken aback when the District Attorney, Anthony Perez, requested a hearing with Mr Carrow at the arraignment, and told him he intended to prosecute me up to the hilt, and even to file further charges. As it states on the court record, I later received a phone call from a person who identified himself as an employee of the Napa County District Attorney's office. He informed me that my prosecution resulted from a deal that had been made with the editor of *The Napa Sentinel*, who maintained an extensive file on the private life of Mr Perez which, if released, would have had a detrimental effect on Mr Perez's chances of filling the vacant position of Superior Court Judge in Napa.

It was a vile campaign by *The Napa Sentinel* against Mr Perez's predecessor that led to Mr Perez's election victory as District Attorney. Knowing about this, and being told by Michael Calhoun that I would never get a fair trial in Napa in front of the Napa County judiciary, made me very fearful. At one point Robert Carrow specifically asked Judge Champlin if he had read *The Napa Sentinel* articles and to our amazement he confirmed he had, but judges are not supposed to read newspaper articles relating to a case in which they are involved lest it bias their impartiality.

Robert Carrow had pointed out to the Assistant District Attorney, and later through motions filed with the court, that the temporary restraining order filed on 13 January of that year was only effective until the time of the hearing of the Order to Show Cause— 31 January. The court had not been asked to extend the temporary restraints beyond 31 January, so had not done so. The earliest that the restraints could have become effective was when the subsequent 15 March order was served on me on 4 April. The mutual restraining order under which I was being criminally prosecuted contained none of the required text that was enforceable anywhere in California by any law enforcement agency. When making the original order, as mandated by law, Judge Snowden, both on the court record and orally, had failed in his statutory duty to inform me what the penalties were for alleged violations of the order. He had also failed to inform me that family members were also covered by the mutual restraining order.

When Robert Carrow filed the motion to dismiss the charges, the time for the District Attorney to file an opposition came and went, and we presumed the DA had given up the ghost. However, we were in for another shock when the District Attorney filed a false proof of service, and instead of Judge Champlin dismissing the case, he allowed things to stand. There was no doubt whatsoever that the court was determined to see a conviction.

An application was again made to Judge Champlin to dismiss the charges as there was no lawful order upon which criminal proceedings could be brought, but it was denied. An application was also made to him to specify what I was alleged to have done, as Robert Carrow and I were having to guess from the plethora of police reports where the prosecution would be coming from at the time of the trial; this was denied. An application was made to have a different judge conduct the actual trial; this too was denied.

One year into the prosecution our investigations turned up three things:

1)    The Assistant District Attorney prosecuting me was a friend of Tess Francis.

2)    Both the Assistant District Attorney and Tess Francis were leaking information to *The Napa Sentinel* to prejudice my chances of a fair trial.

3)    The most shocking discovery of all was that Tess Francis had in the past been a babysitter to Judge Champlin's family. Even then Judge Champlin refused to recuse himself.

There came a point in time when it ceased to be in my interests for Robert Carrow to be my defence lawyer as he had a wealth of information gained while representing me that made him more beneficial as a percipient witness. Consequently, I found myself at the mercy of one of the lawyers in the Napa County Public Defender's Office. Describing this lawyer as useless and hostile would be an understatement. Particularly galling was that he simply failed to communicate with me.

Robert Carrow was in a position to testify at a criminal trial before a jury in many ways. This included the means by which the original mutual restraining order was obtained; the removal of the two declarations from the court file by Judge Bennett; the bias in the Napa County judiciary due to past matters in the case of Cook v. Cook; my reporting Judge Snowden to the Commission on Judicial Performance; the District Attorney's threats to get me; Judge Champlin's actions in thwarting my pretrial motions to stop me getting a fair trial, and so on. If this matter had gone to trial, what would in fact have been on trial was the endemic judicial and extrajudicial malfeasance that permeated and riddled this criminal prosecution. A trial would have been a shambles. The amazing thing was, none of these people realised that what they were doing was totally at odds with the integrity of the entire legal system of the United States. Months previously the Assistant DA had told my defence lawyer that she had tried to withdraw from the case as she thought it was unwinnable, but nobody else in the District Attorney's office would take it on. The trial would anyway, as I have said, been a farce. Tess Francis as the major witness could be impeached at every turn and our intention to call the District Attorney, Assistant District Attorney and Judge Champlin as witnesses would have turned the trial into a media circus.

Finally the Assistant DA was forced to dismiss the charges that had been hanging over me for over two years. My useless public defender lawyer did not even bother to let me know, so the first I knew that the charges had been dismissed was when the Assistant District Attorney told Judge Champlin in open court. Even then Judge Champlin's bias was conspicuous when he refused to let me address the court to declare my innocence.

Appendix 1 (pages 193-195) shows the mutual restraining order upon which I was criminally prosecuted.

# THE WINSTON'S TRIAL

## Chapter 28

I had spent over a year building up a development team to construct Winston's, the British/Irish brew pub, working eighteen-hour days seven days a week. I had secured a lucrative contract with the owners of a retail outlet known as Napa Town Centre where at a certain stage of the pub's development the landlords were to hand over $425,000 towards the construction costs. The Napa Town Centre had a lot of vacant retail spaces and the owners were quite rightly using the proposed creation of Winston's as a lure to attract other tenants. Sadly, all the adverse publicity in *The Napa Sentinel* and the criminal prosecution of me did not sit well with the owners of The Napa Town Centre. It gave them the perfect opportunity to pull out of the deal I had with them, and Winston's shareholders had no choice but to hire lawyers and sue them for breach of contract. For those readers who are not lawyers, there is a vast and succinct difference between Winston's as a corporation with shareholders suing via lawyers, and me as an individual. I was just a shareholder and an officer in the company. In fact, in the State of California a corporation, company or entity can only be represented by a lawyer or lawyers.

To handle the trial on behalf of Winston's I had managed to attract the services of two out of town Napa County lawyers who were not known to each other and who agreed to work together on the trial. Once we all knew that Judge Walker was handling the trial, the first thing the Winston's lawyers did was to formally request he recuse himself as it was well known Judge Walker was a close personal friend of the lawyer representing the defendants. He refused, and things did not bode well as he stated that he did not have much time to hear the trial—he set a maximum of three days—because he was going on vacation. Properly, Judge Walker should have handed things over to another judge. That he did not do so, along with the judge's friendship with a very prominent local lawyer whose son owned a downtown bar with which Winston's would have been in direct competition, provides a classic instance of a case that should not have been heard by Judge Walker, or indeed any local judge, and where an out of county judge ought to have been brought in.

Judge Walker was still not finished with his judicial abuse. As stated, the lawyers representing Winston's were not from Napa County and did not have office facilities there, so as Judge Walker was tweaking the jury instructions to favour the defendants, this required new copies of these instructions to be printed. Subsequently, just before the jury was sworn in, because of these final changes ordered by Judge Walker, a one hour adjournment was required while one of the Winston's lawyers sought printing facilities as a favour from a local law firm. Through no fault of his, one of the Winston's lawyers came back to the courtroom ten minutes over the allocated one hour. For being late, Judge Walker thereupon sanctioned the Winston's lawyer $200 payable to the defendants' lawyer.

As well as fixing the trial by way of the jury instructions, Judge Walker also arranged that critical exhibits could not be introduced into the trial. Therefore, compelling evidence and exhibits were not seen by the jury, nor were they aware of them. Inevitably, the jury came in with an adverse judgment against Winston's, but after they were dismissed, members of the jury came up to our lawyers and me stating they had not wanted to vote as they did but had no choice other than to follow Judge Walker's instructions to them.

For readers not used to trial procedure and the actions of corrupt judges, this award of sanctions was payback by Judge Walker for the Winston's lawyers asking him to remove himself from the case and, more sinisterly, to intimidate the Winston's lawyers lest they were to even remotely step out of line during the trial and challenge any of Judge Walker's ongoing trial decisions. To this day, that sanctioned lawyer has never forgotten Judge Walker's appalling judicial abuse. Of course, had it been a local lawyer being 10 minutes late, there would not have been any sanctions. Fortunately, in all this mess not one person who had invested time or money in Winston's ever threatened to sue me. If they had, life would have become next to impossible as any legal proceedings would have had to take place in Napa County where I would have lost before I even started.

Of course, my dream idea had sunk like a stone.

Losing the trial also marked the end of my relationship with Kelly, once she realised there would be no money forthcoming. We had been together in Sacramento for about eighteen months. It was summer and Graham Jnr was with me, so we had to make alternative plans. I had by now successfully sued Joel Belway in a legal malpractice action for his endless mishandlings when he took over my custody action and the issues resulting from Urie Walsh's conduct. He had not contested it and in fact had done the decent thing and settled, albeit for a nominal sum. I now had a small amount of money left over from the settlement, but I could not go back to living in Napa as the false police reports by Tess Francis would start all over again. By now anyway I was a nervous wreck as I was boxed in on any move I could make. Moreover the strain of the criminal prosecution and the activities of *The Napa Sentinel* had been just too much. What I did was put off the decision about where I was going to live until after the summer. I thought of going back to Katie but this was not an option as her life had moved on: she had not only remarried but had gone to live in her home town in Argentina. I did the only thing I could think of to do, which was to take the Greyhound bus and travel with Graham Jnr throughout the southern United States. At least we would be spending time together as father and son, and in fact we had a lovely summer.

There was a point during our travels at which a twist of fate could have blown me out of the water in regard to the criminal prosecution of me still pending in Napa County. I had decided to take Graham Jnr to Palm Springs in California to show him the Sheraton Plaza Hotel where I had met his mother. When the summer ended and I had returned him to Barbara, I stayed for a short while with friends and just happened to pick up *The Napa Register*. I discovered in the wedding announcements that Tess Francis had got married and had honeymooned in Palm Springs at the exact same time Graham Jnr and I had been there. Had this timing, accidental as it was, been known, I would never have been able to explain it away.

After a while I got a job as a motel maintenance man in Fairfield, just outside Napa.

# VEXATIOUS LITIGANT PROCEEDINGS

Chapter 29

$A$fter the criminal charges had been dismissed I did what most people would do: I sued Tess Francis and her cohorts and, of course, Napa County. Predictably, the defendants hired two large law firms, no expense spared, filing motion after motion. I ended up with three legal boxes crammed to the brim with the documents filed in the pretrial motions, in all of which I had been successful.

It does not take a rocket scientist to figure out that had my lawsuit gone to trial it would have exposed the endemic malfeasance that had gone on in the unjust criminal prosecution of me. *De facto* the Napa County legal system would have been on trial. There were many vested interests, therefore, in doing everything they could to prevent what had happened to me coming before a jury. It was now thirteen years since my son had been abducted and I was still caught up in a nightmare I could not get out of, and been financially wiped out yet again. Like a naive fool I thought Napa County would have settled the action. I had fruitless negotiations with their loss adjuster, which were unproductive because he knew what duplicitous and unlawful trick was lined up to stop me getting to a trial: as their last ditch stand my opponents filed an application with the court to have me declared a *vexatious litigant*. This is a person who files, and repeatedly loses, groundless and/or frivolous lawsuits solely to annoy, harass or subdue an adversary. It is considered an abuse of the legal system.

In civil matters, having a person declared a vexatious litigant is as draconian as the law can possibly get and there are well defined and very strict rules laid down in state law, or by appellate decisions, that are mandatory (appellate courts strive to represent the state's interests

- 164 -

and to advance the rule of law). A judge has to follow the procedures meticulously and the legislated word 'shall' permeates all the instructions and guidelines that a judge has to follow. The person or entity bringing the vexatious litigant application to the court's attention is required in succinct terms to make beforehand what is known as a 'finding'. That means listing all the lawsuits the plaintiff has filed *in propria persona* (where a plaintiff represents him or herself in a legal action without the aid of a qualified lawyer) and where he has not succeeded, giving written reasons for each one as to why the judge concluded that each of the actions provided irrefutable proof that they were lost or unreasonably litigated. What should not happen is listing actions where the claimant was represented by lawyers, was the prevailing party, or not personally involved in the action. It is also important in that the person who has been determined a vexatious litigant can challenge the judge's findings on appeal. Moreover, the vexatious litigation application should be brought at the commencement of the action by the *in propria persona* litigant, not, as in this case, after the defendants had lost various pretrial motions and the action was heading for trial. Not by the wildest stretch of the imagination could I be considered a vexatious litigant. But even though the issue should never have come to court, I had to appear. Happily for me I had attracted the services of an excellent lawyer by the name of Terence Rayner.

In support of their application my opponents dumped into the file, in incomprehensible bundles, over one thousand seven hundred and fifty pieces of paper as exhibits, which by law the judge was required to go through and make a finding on each of them. These consisted of newspaper articles, numerous duplicates, letters, transcripts, documents which I was not even party to, and documents in actions I had filed where they knew I was the prevailing party. About the only bit of paper they didn't file was the county court toilet roll. It would have taken any judge days if not weeks or months to work through the papers, list what was relevant, and separate fact from fiction. In particular they listed eight actions on which they claimed I had litigated *in propria persona* and where I had lost. The success of their claim depended on them showing I had acted repeatedly without a lawyer and had lost. The vexatious litigant statute reads as follows:

*(1) In the immediately preceding seven-year period [the litigant] has commenced, prosecuted, or maintained in propria persona at least five litigations other than in a small claims court that have been (A) finally determined adversely to the person; or (B) unjustifiably permitted to remain pending for at least two years without having being brought to trial or hearing.*

In the eight actions they claimed I had litigated *in propria persona*, two consisted of an action filed by a Californian corporation of which I was only a shareholder. This was listed twice. The important fact about this action is that it was litigated by lawyers, so the action not only did not relate to me personally, it most certainly was not litigated by me *in propria persona*. Another action listed was a lawsuit filed by me against *The Napa Sentinel*, in which I had been successful and which again was litigated by lawyers. There was an action filed by me *in propria persona* against a Redwood bank for libel and defamation, in which again I had been the prevailing party and from which I received substantial financial damages. In fact, the lawyer for the Redwood bank had written to the judge pointing out that I had been the prevailing party and making sure his letter and a copy of the confidential settlement was personally delivered to Judge Christian.

Another action filed by me, allegedly *in propria persona*, was one for conversion (unlawful withholding of property) against Tess Francis. Yet again I had been the prevailing party, the action being litigated by a lawyer, and again the action was dismissed as Tess Francis handed over the documents that she had converted, the very same documents she had previously sworn under the penalty of perjury that she did not have when she obtained the restraining order.

As if that was not enough, they actually included my lawsuit against Tess Francis which of course at this point in time I had not lost! Not only was I now being represented by a lawyer, which anyway brought it outside the criteria for bringing a vexatious litigant motion, but by this time I was prevailing and doing very well. This motion too should not have been listed for a hearing.

The day came for the hearing on the defendants' application to declare me a vexatious litigant, their intention being to dispose of my lawsuit against Tess Francis and the other defendants. I was due to be represented by my Attorney of Record, Terence Rayner, and all the requisite responses had been filed. These raised over thirty points of law as to why their application should not succeed. Due to the sheer volume of paperwork I did not have copies of all the moving papers as they were in the possession of my lawyer. Unfortunately he had fallen sick. He had notified the court of this as well as the team of opposing lawyers. I had spoken to Mr Rayner on the phone and by the sound of his voice there was no doubt in my mind he sounded very ill. Mr Rayner advised me to go to court as a courtesy and confirm to the court that although he was ill he was prepared to make an appearance in a few days' time when he was well again.

As a result of all the turmoil and bitter conflicts that had taken place in the three years since this ordeal started, during which time I became more and more emotionally and physically drained, the Judicial Council of California sent in a retired Californian Appellate Justice by the name of Winslow Christian as a 'neutral' judge. In cases such as this, the 'neutral' judge is expected to bend over backwards to show that he or she is not tainted by any underlying aggravation in the respective county court. Here, however, was a person with a known severe alcohol problem who had once been ejected from a flight from San Francisco to Washington for being drunk. His speech was slurred when he spoke at the hearing and only a drunk could do what he did. He had nothing to lose, being immune from any disciplinary procedures as a retired judge, even though his actions were without doubt criminal in nature. It is a fact that he had sentenced people to long jail sentences for lesser crimes than the conspiracy and fraud that were endemic to the judicial corruption going on here.

I cannot believe there is any judge in the State of California who would even remotely approve of what Winslow Christian did.

As well as my lawyer being ill, I could see that things did not look good for me as I sat on the bench outside the courtroom. I watched Judge Christian arrive and go into the designated judge's chambers, followed a short time afterwards by Judge Bennett. They were together for over twenty minutes. The key fact is that in cases such as this, that sort of thing should simply not happen. There must be neither impropriety nor the appearance of impropriety.

When the court bailiff called the case I entered the courtroom and, significantly, all the files were on the judge's bench, so whatever was going on in the judge's chambers, Judge Christian could not have been studying the files, which he needed to do to come to a fair decision.

The hearing commenced at 11am. When I advised the court that my lawyer was ill and asked that the matter be continued when I could have my lawyer with me, I was given a choice: either I handle the hearing myself or I go to the lawyer's office/home, pick up the papers and come back at 2pm, both of which were impossible options. After I had raised all the requisite objections to not having a lawyer represent me, the judge decided to continue with the hearing.

It is the law in the State of California, settled by repeated decisions, that a party must be heard through his or her lawyer when he or she has one, and the court has no power or authority to recognise anyone in the conduct or disposition of the case *except* the Attorney of Record. What Judge Christian did was simply unlawful and he must have known that. Just the fact that I had a lawyer representing me, by itself negated the application to declare me a vexatious litigant in the action, and was in itself enough to defeat the motion before the court, with or without a hearing. Furthermore, when in desperation I orally made a CCP 170.6 request (that the judge recuse because of possible prejudice and bias), by law Judge Christian was required to adjourn the hearing and submit my CCP 170.6 application to the Presiding Judge of Napa County whose job it would be to determine whether or not he, Judge Christian, was biased. He did no such thing, and carried on.

As the following excerpt shows, my CCP 170.6 rights, which Winslow Christian overruled, are clearly defined by law:

*Since Sec. 170.6 provides for judicial disqualification without any proof of actual bias, once a Sec. 170.6 motion has been filed—together with a declaration under penalty of perjury or an oral statement under oath indicating that the judge is so biased that the moving party or her attorney believes she cannot have a fair and impartial trial or hearing in the matter—the challenged judge ordinarily has no choice but to recuse himself forthwith. Thus, in California, the peremptory challenge right is "automatic" in the sense that a good faith belief in the judge's bias is alone sufficient to insure that the challenged judge will no longer be permitted to sit. In fact, some courts have indicated that when a party properly makes a proper motion under Sec. 170.6, the challenged judge immediately loses jurisdiction, such that any action he thereafter takes in the matter is deemed to be null and void. However, a party's right to disqualify a judge under Sec. 170.6 must be exercised in a timely fashion, and it is well-settled that the challenged judge may himself decide whether the peremptory challenge is timely. In addition, even though motions to disqualify made pursuant to Sec. 170.6 are generally referred to as "peremptory challenges", Sec. 170.6 does require that the movant at least allege that the challenged judge is biased—a fact that has persuaded at least one court to decline to refer to a motion made pursuant to this provision as a peremptory challenge.*

The moment I uttered the words in lines 11-17, page 13 of the court transcript (Appendix 2, page 209), under Californian law Judge Winslow Christian lost jurisdiction and had no more right to try my case than a plumber down the road mending a broken drain. Any litigant in California is entitled to the protection of CCP 170.6 for bias if the judge has not made a finding of fact or the law and this right had not previously been exercised in the action.

The hearing in actual time lasted about ten minutes and at no time when I was there did the judge so much as glance at the files.

As to what followed, we can let an excerpt from the transcript speak for itself. Suffice to say, it clearly indicates an intention on the part of Judge Christian to review the file carefully. I left the courtroom relieved, fully believing he would do as he had said.

THE COURT: . . . *both Counsel are required to submit draft orders in accordance with their views. I'm not indicating that those orders are going to be signed. I am going to review this file with care and study the documentation that is here. If I conclude that, in fairness, oral testimony is necessary and should be taken, I will be vacating the submission and set further hearing [sic].*

Later that day I received a phone call from the bailiff, who advised me that everyone in the courtroom was stunned because, as soon as I had left the courtroom, the defendants' lawyers stepped forward with the prepared orders and, without reviewing one single document in the file, the judge signed them. It was all planned and contrived. What he did was unethical, illegal, criminal, and an abuse of process. In other words he lied to me and all the other people in the court who were not party to his actions. He was no better than a common thief or cheat and I lost a lot of money because of him.

I received the signed order in the mail the next day, as did my lawyer Terence Rayner. I was declared a vexatious litigant and required to post a bond—the size of which I could not meet—if I was to proceed with the lawsuit.

The transcript in Appendix 2 (pages 196-211) shows in full what happened that day in court.

A few days later, Terence Rayner wrote to the court confirming he had been ill and stating his objections to the proposed judgment (see Appendix 3, pages 212-213).

After the hearing at which I was declared a vexatious litigant, two appellate lawyers came to my aid on a *pro bono* basis (they would represent me without charge for their services). The two lawyers were fine lawyers but they metaphorically played the wrong hand. What they did was expend an extraordinary amount of time on the case, with me funding their expenses, to attack and challenge the 1,750 pages of exhibits that Judge Winslow Christian had not bothered to read. Simply put, we were on the wrong motorway (freeway) and heading in the wrong direction. What we should have done was to have kept the appeal simple. All we needed was the court transcript of the hearing, Terence Rayner's letter confirming he was ill, and some simple text in the appellate brief proving the obvious, i.e. Judge Winslow Christian had not read anything and had made a wilfully false statement in open court that he would review all the documents.

With reference to Terence Rayner's legitimate reason for not being present in court, every litigant is entitled to one continuance—an adjournment or postponement to a later date. Where did my appeal end up? As my lawyers got more and more bogged down in preparing the mound of papers required by the court of appeal, they kept asking for continuance after continuance from the California Court of Appeal and missed one deadline after another. The patience of the court of appeal quite rightly ran out and my appeal was dismissed without any of the appellate judges reading a single piece of paper. Yet again I had been let down by the very people who were supposed to be helping me—my own lawyers.

With hindsight we should have just stuck to the issue that Judge Christian had refused to recuse himself and thereby denied me my constitutional and due process right to be represented by a lawyer. As it was, his unlawful action ended with me on public record as a vexatious litigant—my name is still there—with a stain on my character for the rest of my life.

I still have this stigma hanging over me. As the correspondence in Appendix 4 shows (pages 214-217), I have attempted to get this verdict overturned. But even a first year law student would know that what Judge Price wrote in her reply to me on 9 October 2012 is utter bunkum: the presiding judge of a county has the power to remove a person from the vexatious litigant list given certain circumstances i.e. the judge who made the original order is dead or there are extenuating circumstances. There could not possibly be a more specific or mitigating situation than mine. It's not as if I had not sent Judge Price a copy of the transcript of the hearing where I was declared a vexatious litigant, and a copy of Terence Rayner's letter where he confirmed to the now deceased Judge Winslow Christian what I had told the court—that he had been ill on the day of the hearing.

Judge Price has said I can file a new application for permission to file new litigation, but there is no way I am going to put my faith in any justice I would get in the court system of Napa County, California, and get sucked into a bottomless pit of misery again.

My next approach is to send a copy of this book to the Governor of the State of California and ask for a pardon, if that is possible.

# KEEPING A ROOF OVER MY HEAD

## Chapter 30

This might be a good point at which to give you an indication of the hand to mouth way I supported myself, and the sorts of jobs I had to take over the thirteen years I spent in different towns and counties in California where, not by choice, I had to reside. So as to keep a roof over my head, long periods were spent sleeping on friends' or acquaintances' couches or sofas.

My first long-term job in California was with a company that organised conferences; my job was telephone sales, cold calling prospective attendees. In return for cash in hand I got my motel bill paid and also had unlimited use of the phone—essential in keeping contact with my lawyers—which was a great advantage. I could also use the owner's car. One of the owners of this business had another business that I had nothing to do with—selling by consignment, cars that belonged to other persons. One day at these other business premises a dispute took place and my employer was shot by a disgruntled client, which led to the police discovering that there was a warrant out on him in Texas. He was subsequently extradited to serve ten years in the state prison. That was the end of that.

After this I got a job selling hearing aids by telephone cold calling, using the White Pages telephone directory. The problem with this job was not only that it was commission-only, but if the recipient of the phone call could understand the purposes of the call (I was selling hearing aids), logic would dictate they did not need a hearing aid. However, because of the activities of Barbara, Douglas Smith and Urie Walsh, I had to do my best to keep whatever job I could.

Again on a commission-only basis, I tried my hand at selling artwork churned out by an aspiring painter who lived in San Anselmo.

I also tried to put my practical capabilities to use as a handyman but was hindered by not having any money, transport or even tools. This endeavour proved unfruitful after I ran out of acquaintances who needed work doing.

My next job was assisting a woman who owned a failing bakery on Jefferson Street in Napa. I did this job in return for a room in her home, use of her car, and of course food. The problem I had here was that she would not take her failing business seriously by working a regular 9am to 5pm day. We started at any time of the day, which was awkward as I was dependent on her to transport me from her home to the bakery. When we finally got to her business premises I would go out in her car, drumming up new business, which I did well. However, there was difficulty in servicing the new orders as the suppliers were no longer keen to trade with her.

Another difficulty was her refusal to do spot checks on the night shift when the baking was being done, so you never knew what baking was being done on the side and therefore what profits were going into other pockets. As the business imploded, the owner cocooned herself from the bakery's failing state by sinking deeper and deeper into alcohol use and had little or no interest in the business. This was a very unpleasant existence for me as I was treated as a serf and no amount of prompting would get her to face up to what needed to be done. One day the inevitable happened and the bailiffs came, the business went bust and she was bankrupt. If ever there was a business that could have been saved, it was that one.

My job after that was working for a large antique store in Mill Valley. This job was, to say the least, bizarre, as at best the owner could be described as a likeable rogue, otherwise a tax-dodging, eccentric con man. Nonetheless he treated me very fairly, and in exchange for reorganising his shop and business I got a company car, $10 an hour and my motel bill paid. I worked all the hours I could and ran the business fully while he went away on his extensive, long-distance trips abroad where he bought his antiques. For long periods of time I was left to my own devices and given a free hand to refurbish the store, clear out all the junk and restock with better antiques. One of the problems I had with this job, apart from the endemic corrupt practices the owner got up to, was also having to see my employer getting away with routinely fleecing his clients out of simply appalling sums of money (we were located in Mill Valley, Marin County, a very affluent part of California). For example, one afternoon I saw the owner pay $25,000 for a Japanese Samurai sword and the next morning sell it to another client for £475,000. No, I did not get a bonus.

This all came to an abrupt end when I discovered he had been defrauding his major client, who represented 80% of his business, of literally hundreds of thousands of dollars a year, and was involved in exporting antiques in violation of US customs controls, i.e. falsifying their value. I had no choice but to resign lest I came to be associated with what he was up to. This was a major setback for me as I was just beginning to get ahead financially. At her request I went back to living with Katie in Sacramento.

When my relationship with Katie came to a close I ended up working as a motel maintenance man in a place called Fairfield, north of Napa. The manager of the motel had been fired for misconduct. Two women were trying to run the place and were in need of help, so again I did a deal (they did not have the authority to hire me and put me on the books) whereby I would get a room, food, access to a phone and spending money, in return for doing all the maintenance work. In this particular motel you would think you were living in the segregated south because even though rooms were available, these two women would not rent out rooms to black people. When the local health inspector condemned the standard of sanitation of the beds in certain rooms, they would get me to steam-clean a bed in another room and replace the condemned bed with the clean bed, putting the condemned bed back into the other room. Each health inspection would be a game of cat and mouse between the women and the health inspector, the inspector not catching on to their tricks. Sometimes the same rooms were rented out twice a day, with couples engaged in illicit affairs renting the rooms for a few hours, after which the sheets would be cleaned and off we would go again.

This was a lonely and awful job, spending my days bringing each room up to a rentable standard, and at nights and weekends having no money to do anything with in my spare time. This was brought to an abrupt end when the new motel manager arrived. As well as firing the two women, he nailed a notice to my motel room door giving me two hours to leave as I was not officially employed. I had no rights, of course, and so found myself homeless yet again. I managed to get hold of my younger brother, Andrew, in England, who sent me $450, whereupon I worked myself south, back to Napa.

Trying to figure out what to do next, I checked into a cheap motel and sought out a rented room with what little money I had. I applied to a woman I thought had a room to rent who told me she could not help, but had an idea. Her ex-husband had a large home at the Silverado Resort and Spa in Napa; he needed help and could offer an en-suite room. He was severely dyslexic, a massive alcoholic, was involved in a land boundary dispute with his neighbour, had a failing business and was behind on his mortgage. She thought he and I could help each other out, so I arranged to be interviewed and got the position. He was drinking the equivalent of three or more bottles of vodka a day, his business was going out of existence, the mortgage was getting deeper and deeper into arrears and the boundary dispute was overwhelming him. Much as I pleaded with him to give his neighbour the paltry piece of land he wanted, he would not, so the legal dispute just grew and grew.

Things looked more and more bleak and he kept talking time and time again about committing suicide by sitting in his neighbour's pool and shooting himself. I therefore approached a local rancher, Billy Bishop, and asked him, if I removed all the guns from the house, to store them in his gun safe. So having combed through the house and found all manner of guns, I loaded all of them into my employer's car and took them to Billy's, breaking a plethora of laws in the process but feeling I had no choice as I was sure suicide was on the horizon. At least it wasn't going to happen that way.

Bit by bit the world closed in as the business failed and his alcoholism became overwhelming to the point he was living in a parallel universe with the hookers he was renting coming in on a more and more frequent basis as things declined. Even though his behaviour was awful, especially when really drunk, for the most part he was decent to me. But the inevitable happened—the mortgage company foreclosed and I had to get out of the house, along with him.

One day, while I was yet again going from one mundane job to another, I happened to bump into Barbara, who was then working at the Silverado Resort and Spa. She said something to me I have never forgotten, "It's okay for you but my life is over." Talk about hypocrisy! I now didn't own so much as a stick of furniture while she had her own home and never had to worry about a roof over her head.

However, about this time I was in luck as I had won a lawsuit against a local bank because the bank manager had made false statements about me to a local tabloid. Consequently, I had a financial settlement, which meant that for a while at least I could rent my own home, which I did from the woman who had recommended me to this last employer. I was able to buy a car and get some furniture and made extra money painting the homes that this woman owned, although in time obviously the work ran out. As by then my son was sixteen and wanting to do his own thing, I relocated to a converted garage in Mill Valley, just outside San Francisco. This free accommodation was offered to me by the client of the antique dealer I used to work for, who was still grateful for my bringing to her attention the fact she had been defrauded for years. She had obtained a huge financial judgment against him.

The best job I had was providing the public relations and press promotion for the owner of a schooner that did paid excursions around the San Francisco Bay. This required me to organise press articles and free trips for the media. In return for free trips, my job was also to entertain the clients on the trips while the owners sailed the schooner. I was well paid, received a weekly payslip and paid my taxes. I also received free wine and was treated very well by the owner. Sadly, this came to an end because, as much as we all tried, we simply could not make the business pay.

All in all a rag bag of jobs, but they kept me going. Just.

# THINGS YOU NEVER FORGET

## Chapter 31

During the years of court appearances, litigation and precarious living arrangements, I had some experiences that have left me with searing memories of my time in California.

One day I appeared in court on the usual custody matter. At this time my custody action was not only a high-profile case but I was well known to the plethora of judges who had dabbled in it. As I sat at the back of the packed courtroom waiting for my case to be called, I was trying to figure out what was going on at the front of the court. Standing before the judge was a man wearing white overalls, shackled to two guards, and as I was watching people take the stand it struck me I was watching victim impact statements. When that was finished I watched the judge sentence the man to death. After the bit about being taken to the place of execution, and the prisoner was removed from the courtroom, the judge turned to the clerk and said, "I see Mr Cook is in court, let's call his case next." No short recess was allowed for the judge to compose himself after having just passed the death sentence: it was as callous and cavalier as you could get.

Another experience concerns the Embassy Suites Hotel in Napa, which was near to where I had rented a one-bedroom flat. My worldly possessions consisted of a loaned bed, a kitchen stool and a radio. My daily life consisted of going from typing service to typing service in Napa with what little money I had, hoping that one more declaration or filing with the Napa Superior Court would get me some access to Graham Jnr, who was living with Barbara less than a mile away. I was well known at the hotel, as the woman who ran the gift shop had befriended me and, always hungry, I would drop by on a daily basis for a coffee and moral support. One Friday night I was bored, lonely and hungry and could hear music coming from the Embassy Suites Hotel. I dressed smartly and went over there for company. I ordered a coffee, sat at the bar and engaged in very pleasant conversation with a wealthy couple from Texas, exchanging raconteur stories and, as is usual in California, getting free refills to my coffee as this couple ordered their expensive drinks. Still having clothes from when I was once wealthy I did not look broke, and after a period of time the Texan couple insisted I join them for dinner. Although I was hungry I knew with my moral compass that if I accepted their offer of dinner I would be accepting purely out of hunger, so after repeated requests by them I politely declined and left the hotel to go back to my apartment.

After a while I returned to the Embassy Suites and ordered another coffee. At this point I was requested by the bar manager to join him in the atrium. There he told me that everyone at the hotel liked me, but, on a Friday night they calculate that each bar stool nets them $15 in bar sales, and while I was drinking coffee with refills they were not making the sales from that bar stool. In his calculations, however, he had failed to take into account the money the bar had made with my entertaining the Texan couple while they bought their expensive cocktails. Nonetheless, humiliated, I fled the place in tears.

The next morning I received a phone call from the general manager of the Embassy Suites asking if I could come and see him, which I did. What the bar manager said to me had got around the hotel and he wanted to tell me personally he was ashamed at what had happened and, being aware that I was broke, and conscious of the circumstances of my custody action, he offered me their guest complimentary breakfast system whenever I wanted. So, while living at the flat, when I had a court appearance, I would have a free breakfast.

I subsequently could not afford my rent so I was evicted and had to go back to sleeping on friends' couches.

Most police officers will tell you that one of the situations they dislike most is domestic disputes, and I had first-hand knowledge of where their fear came from. I was renting a room in a rundown boarding house in downtown Napa, which was run by the live-in manager and his wife. He had spent time in the state prison and was out on parole. Their rooms were next to mine. One very late Saturday night there was a thump on my wall and a horrendous amount of shouting and screaming and noise coming from their room. I got out of bed to see what was going on. When I looked into their living room the husband was astride his wife, holding a kitchen knife, and the room was wrecked. Even the small air conditioning unit had been thrown out of the window and was hanging by its wire. I interjected and got the man away from his wife, who was about thirty years older than him, and after a while got them to sit at either side of the room. I was aware that if things continued and the police were called, the man would be going back to prison for violating his parole conditions.

After things had calmed down I went back to my room, staying awake in case the disturbance started up again.

The next morning there was a knock on my door and to my astonishment the wife gave me notice to quit, giving me just two hours to leave! I was back looking for a roof over my head on a Sunday morning and asking yet again for someone I knew to put me up on their couch.

In the sticky situation that was my life at the time, there was a further incident which has led me to believe it was not the truth that mattered in court, it was what you could get away with. One day I rented a car for the day, and as I was driving through Napa with my dog Smokey, I shot a red light. The next thing I knew there was a California Highway Patrol car flashing at me and using its loud hailer to order me to stop. At this point in time I was well known in Napa, frequently talking to all and sundry as I took my walks with Smokey as a way of alleviating stress. After I had stopped, the Highway Patrol officer recognised me and profusely apologised to me, stating she had no choice but to issue me with a ticket. I acceded, naturally, and went on my way.

A few weeks later, on a Sunday, I was out walking Smokey again and the same Highway Patrol officer pulled up beside us and asked how things were going, to which I replied I had to go to court the next morning on account of the ticket she had given me. The officer replied that she was off to Hawaii that night and would not be around to testify that she had given me the ticket, which of course meant there would be no evidence against me.

When I turned up in the court the next morning and my case was read out, obviously there was no one to testify against me. When the prosecution and the judge realised this I was asked by the judge how I pleaded, and of course they expected me to say 'not guilty'. Well, I had done what I was accused of so I replied 'guilty', at which the judge again asked me how I pleaded. Everyone again expected me to say 'not guilty' and when I did not they thought I was crazy not to exploit this loophole. Apart from the fact I had done what I was accused of, I had another reason to plead guilty—if I had to appear before this judge in my custody battle, then at least the judge would know I always told the truth . . . what little good that ever did me.

There was one particular incident which would convince most people that you need a good lawyer and how, if you are not a lawyer, you sometimes cannot see the wood for the trees. One day I was in court in a proceeding that I had brought against Harry Martin of *The Napa Sentinel* and, as the moving party, through lack of money I was obliged to represent myself. By pure chance Robert Carrow was in the same courtroom on a totally unrelated matter and in fact he did not even know what I was there for.

I had the owner of the tabloid on the witness stand for over an hour, getting nowhere as he was ducking and weaving and lying through his teeth. As I continued my attempt to cross-examine him, Robert Carrow came from where he was waiting in the public section for his turn to be called, tapped me on the shoulder and instructed me what question to ask next. He continued like this for a while until eventually the judge got fed up with this eccentric performance and said, "Mr Carrow, I have had enough of this. You know better. Either get up here or sit down." Robert Carrow told me to go and sit in the public section and he then stated for the record his name and state bar licence, and said to the judge, "Your Honour, may we forget what we have heard? I have but one question." It was the question I had never thought of asking and involved *The Napa Sentinel's* right to publish legal notices.

The publication of legal notices is a fundamental part of the legal process, i.e. if a person who is party to a lawsuit cannot be located, it is a method of conveying information to that person. California has strict laws regulating which tabloids or newspapers can publish legal notices. The most important regulation is that the newspaper or tabloid must have a certain percentage of its subscribers outside the county or state and the list of subscribers has to be registered with the local United States post office. What Harry Martin did at the hearing was to get caught in his own web of lies. He gave testimony that falsely stated what his general circulation was (thus defrauding his advertisers) and in addition falsely boosted the number of tabloid copies he printed off. I had previously obtained a list of subscribers from the post office, most of whom turned out to be either himself or his cronies or people who lived locally, but, not being a lawyer, had not realised the significance. Robert Carrow simply asked him to restate how many subscribers the paper had and how many copies of the tabloid he printed. Of course, even with the falsely inflated numbers he could not reach the legal requirements, whereupon Judge Walker immediately ruled that *The Napa Sentinel* cease publishing legal notices. When Harry Martin told Judge Walker he had people who had paid him to publish them, the judge simply told him that was his problem. I won my case.

While my life was proceeding as described, I was racking up huge bills, penalties and interest with the Inland Revenue in England. There was no chance of my ever paying them back and, being in California, dealing with all the problems I had there, the Inland Revenue was not my most pressing problem. One fateful day I returned to my studio flat in Tiburon and found three messages on my phone answering machine: two were from lawyers of mine warning me they had been approached by an Inland Revenue private investigator asking where I lived, and the third was from the Inland Revenue private investigator himself, leaving his phone number and asking me to contact him at the Sir Francis Drake Hotel in San Francisco. Deciding it would be best to face up to this problem without any more delay, I immediately phoned the private investigator and agreed to meet with him at 3pm that day at Sam's restaurant in

Tiburon. He was a pleasant enough man and we had a late and amicable lunch on the deck of Sam's, but inevitably he had over two pages of notes for me which had all the tax, penalties and interest that I owed: a huge figure. For a moment as we sat there I thought my luck had changed as there came a gust of wind which, to my glee, blew all his notes into the San Francisco Bay. Determined to single-handedly sort out the UK's economy with the help of all the money I owed, the PI jumped up, ran down the gangplank and offered a man in a rowing boat $20 if he would row him out to pick up the floating notes. When he returned with the soggy notes to our lunch table he said simply, as if nothing had happened, "Now, where were we?"

In the course of our conversation, the Inland Revenue's private investigator told me that in the ten years of his roaming the world looking for people like me, I was the first person ever to call him back; all the others he had had to hunt down. What he offered me was that if I gave him some papers to take back to London to show his masters the mess I was in, he would put in a good word for me. That night we met in the middle of the tunnel under the Golden Gate Bridge and I gave him some legal papers about my custody dispute, after which we shook hands and went our separate ways.

At a later time, when I returned to the United Kingdom I was immediately served with bankruptcy papers by the Inland Revenue. Due to a technicality, my English solicitor got the serving of the papers set aside at a court hearing. Days after the hearing, I received a phone call at my mother's home. It was the head of the Inland Revenue Department asking me to come and meet with him the next day in London. At the meeting I was advised that the best thing I could do, as I was going back to California, was to let them declare me bankrupt. Not only would this clear all my UK debts, they would also apply to have the bankruptcy discharged at the first legal opportunity, which they did. Consequently the bankruptcy had no effect on me.

# TIME TO CALL IT A DAY IN CALIFORNIA

## Chapter 32

After I had obtained joint custody of our son things appeared to settle down. Barbara and I even managed at times to work together on parenting him. One day Barbara told me that Graham Jnr was playing hooky from school and was lying in bed all day demanding she buy him a Tommy Hilfiger jacket. She said she wanted me to take a firm hand with him. At the time he was about fifteen and the only thing I could threaten him with, to which Barbara agreed, was that he would be enrolled in an outward bound school. However, later, she walked me like a fool into a perfect storm.

When Graham Jnr and I were having lunch on the terrace of the Silverado Resort and Spa Country Club he started to tell me he wished that his mother and his grandmother were dead. Of course I did the parental thing and demanded he stop talking like that. He asked to be excused to go to the restroom and didn't come back. Then I noticed Barbara's car pulling up and off he disappeared with her. It transpired that after I had talked to him he had phoned her with quite a different story. This was not unusual, as even throughout my custody battle there had constantly been a problem with my son's manipulative ways and his making up stories.

Weeks went by and I could not get a response from either my son or his mother as to whether he would be coming over to me for his court-ordered summer access. The time came for him to appear, pursuant to this order: he did not turn up. I called Barbara's home over a period of days with no response. Then I phoned his school to see if they knew where he was and was stunned to discover he was attending the school football programme. There were three problems here. My joint custody order specifically precluded Barbara from enrolling him in any programme without my consent and, again pursuant to this court order, she was violating my rights of summer access. Of the various provisions in the court order of 11 April 1991 that Barbara violated, this clause is just one of them:

*The parties shall not make any distractive plans or offer any inducements to Graham Jr that directly or indirectly relate to or infringe upon the other party's rights of defined physical or telephone access.*

The third and major problem was that because he had frequently been playing hooky from school and had poor school grades, state law did not permit him to participate in any school sports programme. Unbelievably, what Barbara and Graham Jnr had done was to falsify the application form. Of course when the school became aware of this they quite rightly ejected him from the programme.

What Barbara and her lawyer did then was to make an application to the court for a court order to force the school to take him back. By California state law, with or without a court order, my son's school could not admit him into the programme, and the newly appointed Superior Court Judge Tisher had no judicial power to order it—no Superior Court judge has the power to ignore or override state law. Barbara and Douglas Smith were either incredibly stupid in bringing such an application to the court or it was the ultimate ploy to turn my son against me. So here I was in court yet again, this time with my son testifying against me, and the judge, trying to mediate, asking me if I would agree to my son going into the school football programme if his grades went up and he stopped playing hooky from school. But as I pointed out to Judge Tisher, the order clearly defined that Graham Jnr would reside with me during the school summer holiday, and his staying with Barbara so as to attend the football programme was in violation of my custody order.

A more experienced judge would have brought massive financial sanctions against Barbara and her lawyer for bringing such an appallingly wrong application to the court. This judge did nothing and it ended in a shambles. I was forced to agree that my son could attend the programme if his grades and also his attendance improved, but as his grades could not go up during the summer vacation, the court order was a charade. This event was probably the straw that broke the camel's back as regards my relationship with my son.

Sometime later Graham Jnr came to my home on what was obviously a fishing expedition and to wheedle money out of me. At this point I had to finally accept the disheartening fact that my son had too many of his mother's genes in him, or, at best, too much of her malign influence.

This was a heartbreaking conclusion given what the whole horrible process had been about. All the recent legal traumas, along with years of having to cope with his and his mother's manipulative ways, led me to realise I could not take the duplicity any more and that I needed to get on with my life. So after more than thirteen years in the shambles of the legal system and the toll it had taken on me, body, mind and soul, I decided to give up trying to make it work in California. I had constantly felt frustrated at having to do jobs well below my skills capacity because it meant I was not doing what I could do best—working for myself. Moreover, I had arrived bright-eyed to start a new life and I was leaving without a penny to my name. Over and above all that, I had lost my children, who were central to my motivation over those years. I had nothing left to lose.

Having said that, I had one thing left that meant the world to me—my dog, Smokey. One way or another Smokey and I were together as constant companions for nearly nine years. Mostly this was when I was with Katie, but also whenever I could have her with me at other addresses. I could not have had a greater help or a more loyal companion while I was living under the enormous stresses that were with me every step of every day.

My intention when I left California was to visit England and then travel on to Spain. I had made some friends in Mill Valley, two of whom had agreed to look after Smokey until I had got established in Spain and who would then arrange her shipment to me. What in fact happened was that one of these persons waited the minimum time in California—thirty days—and formally claimed Smokey as an abandoned dog. By the time I discovered this I was in Spain, and I did not have the money or resources to claim her back. Even if I had the money I was threatened with restraining orders and suchlike if I returned there.

So I had to give up on Smokey and never discovered what happened to my faithful dog. Out of love and respect I decided there and then that I would never have another dog as no other would ever match up to the loyalty and intelligence that Smokey possessed. Her companionship had kept me going throughout those long dark years.

# OFF TO SPAIN

## Chapter 33

Throughout the years I spent trapped in California, I had a romantic dream of one day relocating to Spain and going into business with a former British business colleague who now had a restaurant there. Having finally recognised that I could do no more for my son, and being declared a vexatious litigant, my dream was brought forward. I sold what little I had and travelled to England to stay at my mother's while I made the ongoing plans from there.

After setting my affairs in order in England I flew to Spain where I anticipated starting my life and business career again, using my former colleague as a mentor who would show me the ropes. Unexpectedly, he was not there to meet me. When I arrived at the town where he lived I discovered that he had a new wife, plus a restaurant that was failing. So preoccupied was he with his own problems that he was unable to offer help. I was stranded and did not have a clue what to do or where to turn. I lived in no man's land for weeks, staying in a cheap hotel and looking for employment. I was getting nowhere as the type of work available, such as selling timeshare, was not what I wanted to do. However, I was running out of what little money I had. My luck changed when I saw an advert in the local newspaper publicising a scheme whereby you could obtain funds by cashing in a British private pension. My application was successful and within a few weeks I could look forward to finally having some capital.

Having decided there was no mileage in staying in this small town, I travelled south down the coast to Marbella, being kept afloat financially by my brother Andrew. When I eventually received the money from my British pension fund, I was able to lease a house for a year and, after trying all employment options and finding no satisfaction, decided to spend my time writing a book about my experiences, perhaps as a way of salvaging something from the traumas I had endured. I worked hard at it. By the time I had finished my book, though, I had already decided that living in Spain was not for me. I found myself drinking alcohol at all times of the day and night with people I would not normally drink with, mixing with transient visitors and with people I would not ordinarily socialise with, and I could see where it was all heading. Once my year's lease ran out there was no point in staying. I had given it a go and it was time to move on.

# EPILOGUE

Chapter 34

While living in Spain I developed a friendship with someone who encouraged me and supported my self-belief in thinking I could once again build up a successful new business in the UK. Consequently, I tidied up all the loose ends and returned to England to the village in Oxfordshire where my mother lived. I had no other roots and my Bristol home had long gone. After a time I found a shabby furnished flat to rent, over a shop in the village. As a result of the trauma associated with reliving my experiences when writing the first version of my book (which I had no success in getting published), I was emotionally drained, but I was able to give myself some breathing space before turning my hand and my entrepreneurial brain to the venture where, in spite of everything, I am to this day.

I decided to start a book self-publishing company, namely **WRITERSWORLD**, simply because I could not find any company I thought was capable of publishing the original version that I wrote in Spain. Thus for the last thirteen years I have put all my energies into building up from nothing a successful book publishing company. Initially I borrowed some money from the friend I had made in Spain, but this was soon gone as two local website developers took my money and never delivered the goods. However, I repaid the loan, soldiered on and managed to survive. There were other setbacks when one of my sub-contractors tried to set up in competition in an effort to destroy my business, and a rival company through jealousy launched a false smear campaign. Despite that, my team and I have kept going, developing the company and going from strength to strength. I have built into it the same principles and standard of ethics that I fostered in my early companies. It is only over the last two years or so that I have finally screwed up my courage and managed once again to plunge into those painful Californian memories and produce *11 Oak Street*, one title among many others.

As regards my family, although I am the natural father of my twin daughters, at the present time I have no relationship with them. This is not by my own choice and not for lack of trying, as I have done my best against all the odds. But I was obviously explained away to them by their mother until I have become an unrecognisable caricature of myself in which they have no interest.

I was a dedicated and good father to my daughters, and the sad truth is Jane has never forgiven me for leaving her. What gets to me most is that Ann and Louise now consider that I abandoned them, which in a sense I did when I moved to California when they were eleven. But try as I might, it was impossible to maintain any relationship with them while their mother poured vilification into their ears. I find it hard, though, that later, as well-educated, professional women, they have never stepped forward to find out the truth. I suppose Jane has done just too good a job.

I have no idea where my daughter Ann lives. I know she travelled to California to meet with Barbara and her half-brother, Graham Jnr, so she has been spending time with the woman who had done all she could to destroy her father, though I doubt Barbara allowed her to see it that way.

I managed to locate my other daughter, Louise, but attempts to form any sort of relationship have failed. I know she uses the surname of her stepfather, the man on whom I did the background checks that made such shocking reading. What is the more surprising about this is that when Katie and I met them both all those years earlier in the Canary Isles, it was Louise who told us that the stepfather had molested Ann. I know they think I abandoned them for Graham Jnr. My mother at one time arranged a secret meeting with Ann; what most mothers would have done was use this contact to build bridges, but not mine.

I have no idea where Barbara is living or what she is doing. However, what I do know is that I have sleepless nights realising who and what I married. She has also done a thorough job of brainwashing Graham Jnr.

In my last phone conversation with him on 6 May 2012 he was angry and bitter and told me he believed that when I left California I had abandoned him, and he had no choice but to join the United States Marine Corps. He also told me he had been diagnosed as bipolar and kept going on about all the terrible things he had done in Iraq.

It was a more or less normal son and father phone conversation until he told me he was operating a terrific "scam" and asked if he could come to England and go into business with me so as to operate the "scam" here. To this I replied I already had a business and anyway didn't operate "scams"; then in the time it would take you to click your fingers his demeanour changed and he turned on me. It was like listening to the devil. Off he went, accusing me of blowing a million-dollar condominium in San Francisco. Obviously he has been programmed by his mother and history has been rewritten here as it was his mother who was responsible for the loss of the condominium. Then he let rip with the foulest language, threatening to come to England to cut my mother's and my throat or get his mother's best friend in the Republic of Ireland to put an IRA contract on me. This was the second time this threat has been made against my person, and what on earth my mother had ever done to Graham Jnr is beyond me. I put the phone down on him, after which he left seven ranting messages threatening on each occasion to kill my mother and me.

There is no other way of putting it: because of what occurred, that has been outlined in this book, I literally lost everything. But nothing I could have done differently would have changed matters as regards my children. When you have vengeful parents there is no way of beating that vindictive streak.

As for my mother, the story is as follows. During the war, and prior to my birth, my mother, who was serving in the Women's Royal Air Force, had an affair with a married Royal Air Force officer and became pregnant. The father of this child would not leave his wife, so my mother, who was obliged to leave the Air Force, got a job as a nurse and raised the child. One night she went to a dance and met a very handsome and highly decorated Royal Marine war hero, my father Geoffrey Gordon Cook, who fell in love with my mother at first sight and asked her to marry him. When he proposed to her she responded that they should meet the next day because she had something to show him. When they met she produced her child—my eldest brother. My father was untroubled by this and they went on to marry. This explained the reason for the disparity between the way she treated my brother and me, that is to say, he was the love child. Even so, knowing this did not really explain why my mother was so despising of me throughout my entire life. This I was not to discover until much later.

In my late fifties my mother let slip one sentence that finally explained everything. When talking about the past she said, "If I hadn't been pregnant with you I would have left your father." What I discovered was simply awful. She married my father who, because he loved her, had agreed to raise her first child, and she had another child, this time by my father, so I had two older brothers. One day the father of her first child turned up at her home because he had finally left his wife and wanted to start again with my mother. Of course, she could not leave my father as she was pregnant with me. I guess all her frustration at this state of affairs she subsequently laid on me. Hence my childhood was ruined because my mother married a man she never loved, just to raise her illegitimate son. Well, so be it, people get married for all sorts of different reasons.

Sadly, I have had a lifetime of negatives from her. There was a negative even when I was telling her that I had started the company that published this book—she told me I should get a job as a warehouse man. On my return to England and in these later years as my mother gets older, I almost always go with my younger brother for moral support when I visit her. Where my mother is concerned I simply cannot get away from her subconscious resentment of me because, had she not been pregnant with me she would have left my father and run off with the love of her life.

When she died earlier this year I of course turned up for her funeral and behaved impeccably, strengthened by the fact that she had told all and sundry how good I had been to her during her final years. Although she had been a lousy mother to me I would phone her daily and, apart from normal visits to see her each week, I would in the winter months twice or three times a week travel to Charlbury simply to light the fire and fill the coal buckets. As regards my mother my conscience is clear; I was a good son to her.

I was the last of her sons to see her alive, just one day before she died.

As to Katie, we have maintained a very limited, distant and infrequent contact with each other and on various occasions Katie has stated a desire to come and see me in England, but in my opinion too much water has passed under the bridge for both of us. In this case I think it is best to leave the past to the past.

My domestic circumstances have been an integral part of this story, simply because they were essentially the cause of my crossing swords with the San Francisco and Napa County legal systems. I recognise that I am not alone when it comes to divorce where children are involved. The fallout can be tragic and difficult for all parties concerned, and those who have experienced the worst of it will hopefully be able to empathise with what they have read here. The main thrust of this book, however, has been to expose the malfeasance and disregard for the law, to suit their own ends, by both judges and attorneys, in a legal and judicial system in two counties of the United States of America, of which the founding fathers of that great country would have been utterly ashamed.

Subsequent to publishing this book, my eldest half-brother contacted people who had posted positive reviews about it on Amazon. He made misleading statements to them and asked them to remove their reviews. He himself posted numerous unpleasant Amazon reviews under a false name, in which again he made misleading statements, and was subsequently obliged to remove them.

# APPENDIX 1

---

## THE MUTUAL RESTRAINING ORDER UNDER WHICH I WAS PROSECUTED IN THE TESS FRANCIS TRIAL

AC314

1  NAPA COUNTY LEGAL CLINIC
   LYNN S. YOUNG  CSB NO. 54860
2  ATTORNEY AT LAW
   810 BROWN STREET
3  NAPA, CA  94559
   (707) 257-7333
4

5  ATTORNEY FOR PLAINTIFF

6

7            IN THE SUPERIOR COURT OF THE STATE OF CALIFORNIA
              IN AND FOR THE COUNTY OF NAPA
8                         * * * *

9

10  TESS FRANCIS,                    CASE NO. 68089

11       PLAINTIFF,                  STIPULATED ORDER
                                     AFTER HEARING
12  VS.

13  GRAHAM COOK,

14       DEFENDANT.

15  _____/

16           This matter came on regularly for hearing before the

17  Honorable W. Scott Snowden, Judge of the Napa County Superior Court

18  on January 31, 1994 at 1:30 p.m.

19           Plaintiff, Tess Francis, appeared personally and through

20  her attorney, Lynn S. Young.

21           Defendant, Graham Cook, appeared personally and through

22  his attorney, Robert D. Carrow.

23           The parties agreed and stipulated in open court as

24  follows:

25           1.    That each shall not contact the other, or the

26  other's family members, directly or indirectly, shall not harass,

27  molest or annoy the other, or the other's family members, and shall

28  remain at least 75 feet away from the other and the other's family

                                    1

                                  1525

1    members.  This order does not, however, prohibit Defendant from
2    going to the office of Harry V. Martin so long as he in no way
3    contacts Plaintiff.

4          2.    Plaintiff withdraws all factual allegations in the
5    moving papers in this action.

6          3.    Each party releases the other from any liability of
7    any sort arising from the filing of or response to this action.

8          4.    Neither party will make further reports of alleged
9    criminal violations by the other party in connection with the
10   filing of or response to this action.  This stipulation does not
11   bar either party from reporting any alleged violation of the
12   restraining orders stipulated herein occurring after such orders
13   are made by the court.

14         5.    Upon written application of either party, the matter
15   may be set for review after one year.

16

17   Dated: March 8, 1994            _____
18                                   JUDGE OF THE SUPERIOR COURT

19   Approved as to form and content:
20   Dated:

21

22   _____
     ROBERT D. CARROW
23   ATTORNEY FOR DEFENDANT

24

25

26

27

28

2

1526

# APPENDIX 2

---

## THE COURT TRANSCRIPT WHERE I WAS DECLARED A VEXATIOUS LITIGANT

```
 1    JUNE 9, 1998                        11:00 O'CLOCK A.M.

 2                         --oOo--

 3            The above-entitled matter came on regularly

 4    this day for hearing before the Honorable WINSLOW

 5    CHRISTIAN, Judge Assigned.

 6            GRAHAM COOK, Plaintiff, appeared without

 7    Counsel.

 8            THE LAW OFFICES OF SELLAR, HAZARD,

 9    FITZGERALD, McNEELY, ALM & MANNING, 1111 Civic Drive,

10    Suite 300, Walnut Creek, California 94596, represented by

11    CORIE A. EDWARDS, ESQ., appeared as counsel on behalf of

12    Defendant TESS FRANCIS-TEMPLIN.

13            LONG & LEVIT, LLP, 101 California Street,

14    Suite 2300, San Francisco, California 94111-5895,

15    represented by ZARA J. SANTOS, ESQ., appeared as counsel

16    on behalf of Defendant CALHOUN, KAYFETZ & McINTYRE, a

17    Partnership.

18            DECEMBER MORIN, CSR No. 8718, RPR-RMR, 1001

19    Second Street, Suite 265, Napa, California 94559, was duly

20    present and acting as an Official Shorthand Reporter for

21    the County of Napa.

22            The following proceedings were then and

23    there had and taken, to wit:

24                    P R O C E E D I N G S

25        THE COURT:  Good morning.

26        MR. COOK:  Good morning, Your Honor.

27        MS. EDWARDS:  Good morning, Your Honor.

28        THE COURT:  Please state your appearances for the
```

1    record, moving parties first.

2    MS. EDWARDS:  Corie Edwards of the Sellar Hazard

3    law firm, representing defendant Tess Francis-Templin,

4    moving party.

5    MS. SANTOS:  Zara Santos for defendant Calhoun,

6    Kayfetz and McIntyre, also moving party.

7    MR. COOK:  Good morning, Your Honor.  My name is

8    Graham Cook.  I think you got a message -- I called and

9    left you a message that my attorney called me this morning

10    to tell me he was ill.  And I was told to be here to give

11    you the courtesy --

12    THE COURT:  What is your proposal?

13    MR. COOK:  -- eye to eye.

14    THE COURT:  Do you want to go ahead without Counsel

15    or do you want to wait for Counsel?

16    MR. COOK:  Well, I'd like to do anything to

17    accommodate the Court, Your Honor.  I've got some dates

18    where he can make himself available.

19    THE COURT:  Well, he doesn't know if he's going to

20    be still sick, does he?

21    MR. COOK:  Well, he told me this morning that, you

22    know, he's going to do whatever is necessary.  He didn't

23    expect this to happen.  I wanted the hearing to proceed.

24    I'm supposed to be going to New York on the 16th and I'm

25    supposed to be going to France after that, so I need this

26    thing to go.

27    THE COURT:  All right.  What is his problem today?

28    MR. COOK:  He called me up.  I got back from

1   walking the dog, ready to proceed here to Napa. He has
2   all the papers. And I got a message on my voice mail
3   saying that he had been up all night, he hadn't been
4   sleeping, that he believes he bought a hamburger in
5   Sacramento yesterday that has made him ill, that he was
6   vomiting, so on and so forth, and so on and so forth.
7           So believe me, I was just as shocked and
8   dumfounded. I'm trying to get out of here and go to New
9   York. But, um, so I'm here, Your Honor.
10          THE COURT: Well, we can proceed, if you wish --
11  it's your choice -- without him now, or we can put it over
12  till 2:00 o'clock this afternoon and you can go find him
13  and tell him to be here by 2:00 o'clock.
14          MR. COOK: He's got some dates for Friday, Your
15  Honor.
16          THE COURT: No, we're going to do it today. Today
17  is the day I'm here.
18          MS. EDWARDS: Thank you, Your Honor.
19          MS. SANTOS: Thank you.
20          MR. COOK: But, Your Honor, the problem I have is I
21  don't have any of the moving papers. He has all these
22  papers.
23          THE COURT: Right. But you're going to find him --
24  it's your choice. You can go get the moving papers and
25  proceed by yourself without Counsel, if you want, or find
26  him and tell him that the hearing's been continued till
27  2:00 o'clock this afternoon and he can show up.
28          MR. COOK: Okay.

1    THE COURT:  This is not life-threatening.  A bad

2    hamburger is not life-threatening.

3    MR. COOK:  Well, he did -- sincerely, Your Honor,

4    he did not sound very well to me on the phone.

5    THE COURT:  All right.

6    MR. COOK:  And there was no need for him to --

7    THE COURT:  Is he under medical care?

8    MR. COOK:  I have no idea, Your Honor.

9    THE COURT:  All right.  So far, what I have, is

10   an -- in effect, a truancy.  He's just not here.  He knows

11   that if there's going to be a properly noticed hearing

12   continued for this basis -- on this basis, has to be

13   supported by a showing.

14   MR. COOK:  Well, would a declaration under the

15   penalty of perjury suffice for him?

16   THE COURT:  I would like to look at it.

17   MR. COOK:  All right.

18   THE COURT:  But I would also rather that he came

19   here at 2:00 o'clock and we went ahead with this.

20   MR. COOK:  Well --

21   THE COURT:  I mean, everybody has experience with

22   an occasional episode of food poisoning.  It's a

23   short-term affair.  He should be here at 2:00 o'clock or

24   have a medical certificate.

25   MR. COOK:  Well, may I make a phone call then, Your

26   Honor?

27   THE COURT:  Yes.

28   MR. COOK:  If you can give me a few moments, I will

NAPA COUNTY OFFICIAL REPORTERS - (707) 253-4500

1  try to establish contact with him and put forward your --

2  THE COURT:  Right.  It will be your choice.  If

3  you'd like to proceed now, you can go get the papers from

4  his office and come over here.  That would be your choice.

5  If you don't want to do that and you want him to appear,

6  then we'll put it over to 2:00 o'clock when he can be

7  here.

8  MR. COOK:  That's most gracious of you, Your Honor.

9  THE COURT:  Okay.

10  MR. COOK:  May I make a phone call?

11  THE COURT:  Yes.  So Counsel can just wait here.

12  We'll be in recess here for ten minutes, and you'll let us

13  know the outcome.

14  (Court stands in recess.)

15  THE COURT:  So, Mr. Cook, what have you learned?

16  MR. COOK:  Your Honor, I have just established

17  contact with Terence Rayner, Esquire, who sounds equally

18  as ill as he was.  He is presently in bed.  I have begged

19  and implored and pleaded with him to get here any way, any

20  how.  He says he cannot make it.

21  He has some dates.  One -- I'm sorry, Your

22  Honor.  I don't want to be in this position.  I wanted to

23  proceed with this hearing.  I have worked diligently with

24  him in preparing all the procedural stuff.  He has -- this

25  is the only papers I've got.

26  Some of it I can deal with now, Your Honor.

27  THE COURT:  No, we'll just have one hearing.

28  Do you want to go and get papers from the

1  office and proceed yourself this afternoon?

2      MR. COOK: Your Honor, these are highly complex

3  issues.

4      THE COURT: Just say yes or no.

5      MR. COOK: Will --

6      THE COURT: Do you want to or not? You're not

7  under any pressure. If you don't want to, you can just

8  say that.

9      MR. COOK: Well, Your Honor, if you say to me, do I

10  want to and I say, no -- do I want to leave here and drive

11  all the way down to his place, a house I've never even

12  been to, or an office --

13      THE COURT: I'm taking that as the answer is you do

14  not want to do that.

15      MR. COOK: It's not possible for me to do that,

16  Your Honor.

17      THE COURT: All right. So let's hear some dates.

18      MR. COOK: Your Honor, he said he can be around --

19  he can try and make it -- well, he will make it Thursday

20  morning. All day Friday. Any time, all day Friday.

21      Your Honor, before you do it, I may have a

22  couple of helpful tips here, if I may. I'm just trying to

23  be helpful here.

24      Can I make a couple suggestions?

25      THE COURT: We're talking about dates of hearings

26  right now.

27      MR. COOK: Oh.

28      THE COURT: The possibility exists of doing this

1    on --

2           MR. COOK:  Thursday morning.

3           THE COURT:  No.  I can't -- I have other dates --

4    times set.

5                 The one that would be available is Monday,

6    the 15th, in the afternoon.  2:00 o'clock on the 15th.

7           MR. COOK:  Can I borrow a pen from somebody?  I'm

8    sorry.

9                 Monday the 15th.

10          THE COURT:  Moving parties, how does that work for

11   you?

12          MS. EDWARDS:  Your Honor, we would like to oppose

13   any grant of a continuance.

14                These motions have been fully briefed.  They

15   have been pending on the court calendar since February of

16   this year.  The statutory provisions under the anti-slap

17   statute entitle our clients to production of that slap

18   statute, which requires the hearing to be held within 30

19   days after filing of the motion.

20          THE COURT:  Right.  So you're asking me to proceed

21   with an unrepresented party, over his objection; is that

22   the idea?

23          MS. EDWARDS:  No, we're not.

24          THE COURT:  Okay.

25          MS. EDWARDS:  Your Honor, we don't believe that

26   oral argument is even necessary on this hearing, given the

27   extensive legal briefing that has been filed on behalf of

28   both parties.  Mr. Cook did file a late opposition that

1    was signed by his attorney, so his attorney has had the

2    opportunity to bring to the Court's attention any

3    arguments that he feels need to be made.

4         THE COURT:  The statute does permit 391.2 at the

5    hearing, and this is the properly noticed time for the

6    hearing, I'm taking it.  The Court may consider such

7    evidence, written or oral, by witnesses or affidavit as

8    may be material to the ground of the motion.

9              And so you're proposing that it be submitted

10   for decision based on the written showings that have been

11   made?

12        MS. EDWARDS:  We are.  The language that I was

13   referring to is fully contained in the anti-slap statute,

14   which is CCP 425.16.  I believe that this --

15        THE COURT:  Well, that statute does not override --

16        MS. EDWARDS:  Okay.

17        THE COURT:  -- constitutional rights.  I mean, what

18   is your view, ma'am?

19        MS. SANTOS:  We concur with their position as well.

20             The papers have been submitted.  This

21   hearing has been noticed for a long time.  The

22   substitution of attorney we only received yesterday.  The

23   reply briefs, their opposition, were late, and we would

24   like those not to be considered.

25             We basically perceive this as another way of

26   delaying --

27        THE COURT:  Well, I don't know that.

28        MS. SANTOS:  -- this resolution.

1      THE COURT: Now what I'm going to do is I'm going

2  to listen to Mr. Cook first. But the proposal is to take

3  this under submission, including the late filing. It just

4  doesn't make sense to refuse to receive information when

5  we're talking about a submission on papers.

6      MS. EDWARDS: Okay.

7      THE COURT: Mr. Cook?

8      MR. COOK: Well, Your Honor, that does violate my

9  due process equal protection rights.

10      THE COURT: Okay. I want to hear from you about

11  that.

12      MR. COOK: Well, I don't have -- I don't have all

13  the points, and I'm not an attorney.

14      THE COURT: Um-hmm.

15      MR. COOK: And I don't wish to be an attorney. But

16  there are a couple of problems here, and let's try and see

17  if I can recollect some of the procedural difficulties.

18      THE COURT: No, no, no. I want to hear about

19  the -- whether there's a -- whether your showing is true,

20  the showing that you've made in this opposition.

21      MR. COOK: I'm saying to you, Your Honor, if we're

22  not allowed to proceed --

23      THE COURT: You are allowed to proceed.

24      MR. COOK: -- taking oral testimony --

25      THE COURT: You're declining to proceed?

26      MR. COOK: No. I had -- I had witnesses lined up

27  here as well, three -- the vexatious litigant statute

28  gives me the right for oral testimony.

1    THE COURT:  No, it does not.

2    MR. COOK:  At the Court's discretion.

3    THE COURT:  Yes.

4    MR. COOK:  And I had an attorney ready to come and

5    testify here this morning, an attorney that has spoken to

6    Ms. Edwards.  His name is Erik Nordguard.  And Erik

7    Nordguard was going to appear here this morning at 11:00

8    o'clock.  I called him this morning and told him not to

9    come.

10    And he was going to tell you, Your Honor,

11   under the penalty of perjury, that Miss Edwards has

12   extended this mutual restraining order in the underlying

13   for another three years.

14    THE COURT:  We're not going to get into all that.

15    MR. COOK:  Well, that's --

16    THE COURT:  If you have any brief statements you'd

17   like to make for the record, you may proceed.

18    MR. COOK:  Okay.

19    THE COURT:  But it needs to be a brief statement.

20    MR. COOK:  Your Honor, I strongly think it

21   inappropriate, with all due respect, to proceed without me

22   being represented by Counsel and without oral testimony,

23   and I'd like to make the issue of the statutory -- or the

24   constitutional and due process rights.

25    There was two motions filed, the two motions

26   on calendar.  Those motions were filed at the Marin County

27   Superior Court when, one, the moving party was in default,

28   two, a motion was on calendar for change of venue, and the

1  venue had been changed.  I stood in Judge Thomas'

2  courtroom at Marin County Superior Court and I heard Judge

3  Thomas order Sellar-Hazard and these defendants not to

4  file anything in Marin County Superior Court.

5          Furthermore, the anti-slap one also requires

6  a motion to be brought within 60 days with -- with leave

7  of the court, but it also requires that the hearing be

8  held within 30 days.

9          When they filed these motions, Your Honor,

10  at the Marin County Superior Court, when they were in

11  default, when there was a change of venue motion, the

12  judge had ordered the change of venue, they set the

13  hearing for March the 6th.  They knew that they could not

14  look -- comply with 421.G and have the hearing within 30

15  days.

16          We now move on to another issue, Your Honor,

17  which is right back on my constitutional rights.  391, the

18  vexatious litigant, gives me the right to, in fact, call

19  witnesses, oral testimony, or to request the Court of

20  that.  The anti-slap one stays all discovery.  The burden

21  on these people is to prove, on February the 13th, which

22  one of those two motions was filed first.  Because if they

23  filed the anti-slap motion, they violate my constitutional

24  rights to have witnesses to testify in the vexatious

25  litigant motion.  If they filed the vexatious litigant

26  motion first, Your Honor, they could not have filed the

27  slap motion because vexatious litigant stays all

28  litigation.  You cannot have your cake and eat it, and

1   this was done to willfully process the Court.

2             Now, also, they haven't filed an answer.

3   They filed the answer to the Complaint when they were in

4   default.  So we have 31 procedural points that the lawyer

5   has worked on, 31 of them, before we even get to the

6   merits of the case.

7             THE COURT:  Well, the way it goes is that there are

8   two motions pending by them.  They are the moving parties.

9   If we were having a merits hearing on this, we'd hear from

10  them first in support of their motion.  But the statute

11  does not require they bring evidence -- oral testimony be

12  taken, and so I'm ordering both motions submitted for

13  decision based on --

14            MR. COOK:  Well, Your Honor, I need to put on the

15  record --

16            THE COURT:  -- based on the showing that has been

17  made.

18            MR. COOK:  Now, Your Honor --

19            THE COURT:  Now I'm asking that you remain silent,

20  sir, because I have a further order to make.

21            Both Counsel are requested to submit draft

22  orders in accordance with their views.  I'm not indicating

23  that those orders are going to be signed.  I am going to

24  review this file with care and study the documentation

25  that's here.  If I conclude that, in fairness, oral

26  testimony is necessary and should be taken, I will

27  vacating the submission and set further hearing.

28            MR. COOK:  That --

| | |
|---|---|
| 1 | THE COURT: And the hearing is adjourned. Court is |
| 2 | adjourned. |
| 3 | MR. COOK: Your Honor, may I lay a bit more of a |
| 4 | record? |
| 5 | THE COURT: All right. Carry on. |
| 6 | MR. COOK: I mean, Your Honor, I'm just trying to |
| 7 | do the right thing. I have a proposed stipulation on the |
| 8 | vexatious litigant motion. Will you look at that |
| 9 | before -- |
| 10 | THE COURT: No, sir. |
| 11 | MR. COOK: Okay. Then I'd like to formally enter |
| 12 | 170.6, if I may, Your Honor. |
| 13 | THE COURT: No. It's too late for that. |
| 14 | MR. COOK: You haven't made a finding of law, Your |
| 15 | Honor. |
| 16 | THE COURT: That challenge is disallowed. The |
| 17 | hearing is adjourned. |
| 18 | MR. COOK: Thank you, Your Honor. |
| 19 | MS. SANTOS: Thank you, Your Honor. |
| 20 | THE BAILIFF: Your Honor, I was just given these to |
| 21 | give to you. |
| 22 | THE COURT: I beg your pardon? |
| 23 | THE BAILIFF: I was just given these to give to |
| 24 | you. Is that appropriate? |
| 25 | MS. EDWARDS: Those are the proposed orders. |
| 26 | THE COURT: All right. I'd like to have that. |
| 27 | MS. SANTOS: Your Honor, we also submitted proposed |
| 28 | orders with our papers already. |

1          THE COURT:  All right.  Thank you.  Hearing is
2    adjourned.
3                    (Proceedings were concluded.)
4                         --oOo--
5
6
7
8
9
10
11
12
13
14
15
16
17
18
19
20
21
22
23
24
25
26
27
28

```
 1   STATE OF CALIFORNIA )
                        )  ss.
 2   COUNTY OF NAPA      )

 3

 4            CERTIFICATE OF SHORTHAND REPORTER

 5

 6            I, DECEMBER MORIN, CSR No. 8718, RPR-RMR,

 7   Official Shorthand Reporter for the County of Napa, do

 8   hereby certify:

 9            THAT on Tuesday, June 9, 1998, I reported in

10   shorthand writing the proceedings had in the case of

11   GRAHAM COOK versus TESS FRANCIS-TEMPLIN, et al., No.

12   26-01469.

13            THAT I thereafter caused my said shorthand

14   writing to be transcribed into longhand typewriting.

15            THAT the foregoing pages 1 through 14

16   constitute and are a full, true, correct and accurate

17   transcription of my said shorthand writing, and a correct

18   and verbatim record of the proceedings so had and taken,

19   as aforesaid.

20            DATED this 23RD day of JUNE, 1998.

21

22

23

24                          DECEMBER MORIN
                            CSR No. 8718, RPR-RMR
25                          Official Shorthand Reporter
                            County of Napa,
26                          State of California

27                               --oOo--

28        CERTIFICATION OF THIS TRANSCRIPT IS VALID ONLY
               WITH AN ORIGINAL SIGNATURE.
```

NAPA COUNTY OFFICIAL REPORTERS - (707) 253-4500

# APPENDIX 3

---

## LETTER FROM MY LAWYER TO THE COURT CONFIRMING HIS ILLNESS AND STATING HIS OBJECTIONS TO THE PROPOSED JUDGMENT

TELEPHONE
(415) 468-9116

P.O. BOX 85 / 300 ARROYO
LAGUNITAS, CALIFORNIA 94938

June 21, 1998

The Honorable Winslow Christian
Assigned Judge of the Napa Consolidated Courts
c/o Ms. Judy Link, Court Services Supervisor
Superior Court of California, County of Napa
825 Brown Street
Napa, CA 94559-0880

Re: Cook v Templin et al
    Case No. 26-01469

Dear Judge Christian:

I received in the mail today a copy of a letter addressed to you
along with a proposed judgment in this matter.

I have a number of objections to the proposed judgment submitted
by Ms. Edwards.

Neither the previous order or this proposed judgment was
submitted to me for approval as to form. Neither was a proposed
order forwarded to Mr. Cook at the time the moving papers were
filed which is required. The California Rules of Court require
all of the above.

Since I was not present due to an illness of which I notified
both the court and all of the attorneys early the morning of the
hearing, I was not aware of what exactly occurred, other than Mr.
Cook was apparently forced to go forward on the hearing without
me. I do understand that the matter was taken under submission
by you, although I note that the Orders were signed the same day
and mailed the same day.

The proposed judgment does not conform with the order you signed.
It also contains additional language in paragraph 1 that requires
Mr. Cook to post a bond before he can file a motion for
reconsideration or appeal in this matter. This is improper.

Very truly yours,

Terence Rayner

cc    Corie Edwards
cc    Zara Santos

# APPENDIX 4

---

**MY CORRESPONDENCE WITH THE PRESIDING JUDGE
REQUESTING TO BE REMOVED FROM THE LIST
OF VEXATIOUS LITIGANTS IN CALIFORNIA**

Graham Cook

The Honourable Diane M. Price
*Presiding Judge*
Superior Court of the State of *California*
*County of Napa*
825 Brown Street
*Napa*                                                July 26, 2012

*CA* 94559
United States

**Reference: My official request to be removed from the list of Vexatious Litigants in the State of California as declared in Case Number 26-01469.**

Dear Judge Price,

I attach for your attention a copy of an e-mail message from your colleague which contains a factual error; my letter to you was a formal request as permitted by statute, not an informal request.

With respect it is difficult to imagine any situation where the legislature of the State of California could be deemed more suitable for a vexatious litigant to be able to write to the Presiding Judge of a county requesting removal, considering:

- ❖ the corrupt circumstances where I was declared a vexatious litigant
- ❖ the passage in time
- ❖ no subsequent actions filed
- ❖ the fact that I no longer reside or intend to reside in the State of California
- ❖ and as your own local newspaper recently states, a shortage of Judges in your county and the waste of courtroom time and needless expense in filing a formal application with the court.

May I ask again that you grant me the legal relief the legislature of the State of California intended when they enacted the vexatious litigant statute.

Yours most respectfully,

Graham Cook

C.c. *Judge Francisca* P. *Tisher*

# Superior Court of California
# County of Napa

Judges
Diane M. Price
Rodney G. Stone
Francisca P. Tisher
Mark Boessenecker

Commissioners
Michael S. Williams
Monique Langhorne-
Johnson

Court Executive Officer
Richard D. Feldstein

October 9, 2012


Graham Cook




United Kingdom


Re: Correspondence


Dear Mr. Cook:

I am in receipt of your July 27, 2012 letter asking that I remove you from California's vexatious litigant list. Pursuant to California code of Civil Procedure, section 391.8, you must file a formal application for such relief. The application may be filed either in Napa Superior Court case number 26-01469, or as a separate application for permission to file new litigation, as set forth in section 391.7.

I will not be taking any action based upon your correspondence.

Telephone
(707) 299-1100

Historic Courthouse
625 Brown Street
Napa, CA 94559-3031
FAX: (707) 299-1250

Criminal Courthouse
1111 Third Street
Napa, CA 94559-3001
FAX: (707) 253-4673

Juvenile Courthouse
2350 Old Sonoma Road
Napa, CA 94559-3703
(site address only –
no mail delivery)

Diane M. Price
Presiding Judge
Napa Superior Court


DMP/ymo

Graham Cook

The Honourable Diane Price
Presiding Judge
Superior Court of the State of California
Phone: 01993 812500
County Of Napa
825 Brown Street
Napa,
CA94559
United States                                    October 20, 2012

**Reference: My official request to be removed from the list of Vexatious Litigants in the State of California in case number 26-01469**

Dear Judge Price,

I was somewhat surprised at the content of your letter to me which does not reflect the law as I understand it, and also the fact that all my correspondence was returned to me. With respect, this was a needless waste of public money as naturally I have copies of all that I sent you.

As I intend to report your conduct to the Commission on Judicial Performance, I am returning to you what you sent back to me, and request that all this material be placed on the public record.

I shall of course incorporate your letter to me, and also this letter, in my forthcoming book, so others may be the judge of how this matter has been handled.

Yours respectfully,

Graham Cook

Printed by: Copytech (UK) Limited trading as Printondemand-worldwide, 9 Culley
Court, Bakewell Road, Orton Southgate, Peterborough, PE2 6XD